Contents of Read Instantly

200 Phonics Lessons for all Ages

In this book, over 180 spelling patterns of the sounds we call phonics are placed in a queue and then introduced logically, one-at-a-time, and in a group 20 to 50 words.

Symbols & Concepts Used	V
Teaching Instruction	1

1 — Short Vowels, Double Consonants, Silent Letters, Consonant Blends

Lesson 1: Read the names of the 26 English letters	5
Lesson 2: Read the first sound of each letter	6
Instruction to Teachers or Tutors	7
Lesson 3: Short vowels in 180 words, each vowel has a unique short sound	8
Lesson 4: There are double letters in English, as in "i**nn**"	12
Lesson 5: The **ss**, **ff**, **ll**, **zz** come in doubles at the end of short words	12
Lesson 6: There are silent letters in English, as in "bom**b**"	13
Lesson 7: Introducing the consonant blends, as in "**dr**ess"	13
Lesson 8: Compare the five short vowels in 171 essential words	15
Teaching Instruction	18

2 — Introduction to Long Vowels and two Vowels Spelling Rules

Lesson 1: Two vowels walking Rule: r**āi**n, m**ēa**t, t**īe**, b**ōa**t, bl**ūe**	19
Lesson 2: The **a-e** can still walk Rule: f**ā**t*e*, P**ē**t*e*, b**ī**t*e*, h**ō**p*e*, t**ū**b*e*	22
Teaching Instruction	26

3 — Inconsistent Consonants: y, h, c, g, q, x, s, ve, ac

Lesson 1: The "**y**" as a vowel: m**y**, cit**y**, d**ay**, b**oy**, g**y**m	27
Lesson 2: The **11** digraphs of **H**: **sh**ip, **th**is, **th**ink, ea**ch**, s**ch**ool, **ch**ef, **ph**oto, **wh**o, **wh**en, ri**gh**t, tou**gh**	29
Lesson 3: The soft and hard **C**	33
Lesson 4: The soft and hard **G**	38
Lesson 5: The **S** that sounds like a **Z**	43

I

Lesson 6: The **Q** sounds like a **K**	45
Lesson 7: The **X** sounds like **Ks** or **Kc**	47
Lesson 8: Adding a final "**s**" or "**es**"	50
Lesson 9: The final **-ve**, the prefix **ac-**	52
Reading Aloud is Imperative	53
Teaching Instruction	54

4 — Affixes: tech-, -some, -cal, -tion, -cle, and ătt

Lesson 1: The affixes **tech-**, **-some**, **-cle**, **-cal**	55
Lesson 2: The suffixes: **-tion**, **-sion**, **-cian**	57
Lesson 3: Doubling the consonants after the short vowels (ătt, ĕpp, ĭnn, ŏbb, ŭgg)	58
Teaching Instruction	62

5 — The 5 Sounds of the Vowel A are Spelled in these 12 Ways

Lesson 1: The **five** sounds of "**a**" are spelled in **12** spelling patterns	63
Lesson 2: The short **ă** as in "m**a**n"	64
Lesson 3: The long **ā** sound is spelled in these **five** ways:	65
1 **āy** as in "d**ay**" 65 **2** **āi** as in "r**ai**n"	66
3 **ā-e** as in "**ate**" 67 **4** **ā** as in "**a**ble"	68
5 **ei** as in "**ei**ght" 69	
Lesson 4: The special sounds of "**a**" spelled in these **five** ways:	70
1 "**all**" as in "**all**" 70 **2** "**al**" as in "**al**ways"	71
3 "**aw**" as in "dr**aw**" 72 **4** "**au**" as in "**au**to"	73
5 "w**ar**" as in "w**ar**m"	74
Lesson 5: The weak sound of "**a**" as in "li**a**r"	75
Teaching Instruction	76

6 — The 4 Sounds of the Vowel E are Spelled in these 17 Ways

Lesson 1: The **four** sounds of "**e**" are spelled in **17** spelling patterns	77
Lesson 2: The short **ĕ** sound spelled in these **two** ways:	78

Contents

| 1 ĕ as in "br**e**d" | 78 | 2 ĕ as in "br**ea**d" | 79 |

Lesson 3: The long ē sound spelled in these **10** ways: 80

1 "**ee**" as in "m**ee**t"	80	2 "**ea**" as in "m**ea**t"	81
3 "**e-e**" as in "P**e**t**e**"	82	4 "**i-e**" as in "**e**l**i**t**e**"	83
5 "**ie**" as in "ch**ie**f"	84	6 "**ei**" as in "rec**ei**ve"	85
7 "**ey**" as in "k**ey**"	86	8 "**y**" as in "cit**y**"	87
9 "**e**" as in "h**e**"	87	10 "**i**" as in "sk**i**"	88

Lesson 4: The weak sound of "**e**" as in "cem**e**tery"   89

Homework   90

7 The 8 Sounds of the Vowel I are Spelled in these 19 Ways

Lesson 1: The **eight** sounds of "i" are spelled in **19** spelling patterns   91

Lesson 2: The short ĭ sound is spelled in these **two** ways: 92

| 1 ĭ as in "J**i**m" | 92 | 2 ĭ as in "g**y**m" | 93 |

Lesson 3: The long ī sound spelled in **10** ways: 95

1 "**-y**" as in "m**y**"	95	2 "**igh**" as in "h**igh**"	96
3 "**ign**" as in "s**ign**"	97	4 "**i-e**" as in "f**i**l**e**"	98
5 "**y-e**" as in "st**y**l**e**"	99	6 "**i**" as in "h**i**"	100
7. "**y**" as in "c**y**cle"	101	8 "**i+ semivowel**"	102
9 "**ie**" as in "d**ie**"	103	10 "**ye**" as in "d**ye**"	104

Lesson 4: The special sounds of "**i**" as in "so**ci**al"   105

Lesson 5: The weak sound of "**i**" as in "test**i**fy"   106

Homework   106

8 The 12 Sounds of the Vowel O are Spelled in these 20 Ways

Lesson 1: The **12** sounds of "o" are spelled in **20** spelling patterns   107

Lesson 2: The short ŏ as in "h**o**t"   108

Lesson 3: The long ō sound spelled in **nine** ways: 109

1 "**oa**" as in "b**oa**t"	109	2 "**oe**" as in "J**oe**"	110
3 "**ou**" as in "f**ou**r"	111	4 "**o-e**" as in "h**o**p**e**"	112
5 "**ow**" as in "sn**ow**"	114	6 "**o**" as in "g**o**"	115

III

7 "o + semivowel" — 116
8 "ōy" as in "boy" — 117
9 "ōi" as in "boil" — 118
Lesson 4: The special sound of "o" as in "now" and as in "noun" — 119
Lesson 5: The minor sounds of "o": wood, one, touch, ought — 121
Lesson 6: The weak sound of "o" as in "favor" — 122
Homework — 122

9 The 6 Sounds of the Vowel U are Spelled in these 28 Ways

Lesson 1: The **six** sounds of "u" are spelled in **28** spelling patterns — 123
Lesson 2: The short ŭ as in "up" — 124
Lesson 3: The long ū sound spelled in these **eight** ways: — 126
1 "ue" as in "blue" — 126
2 "ui" as in "suit" — 127
3 "u-e" as in "cute" — 128
4 "eu" as in "feud" — 129
5 "o" as in "to" — 132
6 "oo" as in "zoo" — 133
7 "ou" as in "you" — 134
8 "oo" as in "book" — 134
Lesson 4: The special sounds of "u": cul**ture**, liq**u**id, g**u**est, b**u**siness — 135
Lesson 5: The weak sound of "u" as in "vir**u**s" — 136
Lesson 6: Review of old and new phonics — 137

10 Writing the ABC's

Lesson 1: Now is the time to write the **ABC's** — 139

The **10** Phonics-based Spelling Books for all Ages by Linguist Camilia Sadik — 145

Symbols & Concepts Used in this Book

Silent letters are italicized in this book, like the silent *p* in recei*p*t.

Dots inside words indicate divisions of words into syllables, as in win·dow.

Vowels are **a**, **e**, **i**, **o**, **u**, sometimes **y** as in sk**y** and sometimes **w** as in fe**w**. Vowels rule English and they cannot be avoided. Vowels change drastically; they make **38** sounds we call phonics, which are spelled in **96** ways we call spelling patterns. To learn all the changes in the vowels, Linguist Camilia Sadik dissected and isolated each vowel it in a book.

Consonants are the rest of the letters. Vowels are very inconsistent and the eight consonants c, g, h, q, s, x, w, and y are also inconsistent. The eight inconsistent consonants are isolated in a book; they produce **50** sounds, which are spelled in **60** ways.

A syllable is a part of a word, like "me" in "me·di·a" or a small word, like "me" that contains only one vowel sound. There are two syllables in "win·dow." There are three syllables in "b*eau*·ti·ful." There is one syllable in "stopp*e*d." A syllable may contain more than one vowel but it can only have one vowel sound.

A schwa is a weak sound of any vowel, as in sep·**a**·rate, sou·v**e**·nir, sol·**i**·tude, mem·**o**·ry, and vir·**u**s. Other syllables may be stressed, but not the syllables where the schwa is.

A Phonic is a single sound produced by a number of letters, like "**ture**" in "cul**ture**" or by a letter that does not sound like its letter name, like "**o**" in "ch**o**ir."

Semivowels are l, m, n, r, and s. Vowels have sounds and consonants are soundless unless they are said with a vowel. However and in spite of being consonants, the semivowels have some sounds of their own, even when not said with vowels. Moreover, these five consonants have various effects on the vowels that precede them; and sometimes, they act like vowels. They may make the preceding vowels long, as in ch**i**ld, c**o**mb, r**a**nge, p**o**rt, and p**a**ste. For this reason, the author granted the name semivowels to these five consonants.

Reading aloud is imperative and there are details about reading aloud in the *Teachers' Guide*. Learners must read aloud all the practice lessons in these books. If reading silently, students will understand the rules but will not memorize the spelling of words.

Logical learning style: English words were not written for logical learners who need logic before they can memorize. In English, one needs to memorize without logic which spelling pattern of a sound to choose when spelling every single sound in every English word. Logical learners are analyzers who question the logic behind spelling English words one-way and not the other. They simply cannot memorize without logical spelling rules to show them when to spell a sound one-way and not the other.

Dyslexic persons are logical learners; they need logical spelling rules before they can memorize the spelling of words. However, dyslexia in spelling and in writing letters in reverse does end, after learning to spell and after slowing down to write words slowly.

Dyslexic persons **cannot focus on both** reading comprehension and on the way, words are spelled; they can only focus on one thing at a time. While teachers may think, every child in the classroom is reading a story and looking for the main idea, kids whose learning style is a logical learning style are pausing to question, why "M*y* c*at* i*s* c*u*te isn't M*i* k*at* i*z* q*u*t?" Pausing to question causes them to fall behind in class.

Dyslexia in spelling: Understanding dyslexia is the key to ending it. Read "How do you get dyslexia?" by Camilia Sadik, and you will agree that dyslexia is given to kids before the 3rd grade. Forced speed-reading before learning to spell words causes dyslexia in spelling. When kids are forced to hurry, their vision travels rapidly from left-to-right and vice versa. In their haste, they see letters in reverse. When writing, they also hurry and write letters in reverse, in the same manner that they saw them and read them.

ADD can end: Most cases of ADD are due to boredom from sitting in class and not learning. When dyslexia ends so does ADD that is caused by dyslexia.

ESL students learn to speak, read, spell, write, and become literate in English in 400 to 500 hours of studying or supervised instructions, depending on their levels. At the start, they specifically benefit from *Read Instantly* and from *English for Non-native English Speakers*. At a later stage, they benefit from the rest of the books. ESL students can learn to read from *Read Instantly* even if they do not speak English; they read phonics similar to the way they read the ABC's.

Sadik's books are **for all ages and all types of learners.** All benefit from these comprehensive phonics-based reading and spelling books. They are ideal books for K-12 parents or teachers and for adult learners from diverse backgrounds.

For sample lessons and much more, visit us at **SpellingRules.com**

Teaching Instructions

Step 1 Follow the order of the lessons presented in this book, as each step is planned carefully and no lesson is placed here arbitrarily. Initially, over 180 spelling patterns, of the various English sounds we call phonics, are placed in a queue awaiting their turn to be introduced logically, one-at-a-time, and in groups of words.

Step 2 Chapter 1 begins by showing students how each consonant sounds and how it differs from its letter name when used in words. Make the sound of the name of the letter "**h**" (ai+ch), and then tell students that as in "**h**at" the "**h**" sound differs when used in words.

Step 3 At the start, a letter with a sound that is very different from its letter name is avoided. For instance, the "**q**" sounds like a "**k**" and needs to be avoided until it reaches its turn in the queue.

Step 4 Adhere to the Informing Before Introducing Approach (IBIA) used throughout this book. Most students who have just learned the ABC's expect each letter to sound like its letter name when used in words. For instance, they are unaware that the "**q**" makes a "**k**" sound unless they are informed beforehand and shown enough examples.

Step 5 Pay attention to students with a Logical Learning Style: English was written for memorizers, but logical learners cannot memorize without logical explanations as to why a sound should be spelled one-way and not the other. Students with a logical learning style question why they are told one thing and then asked to read another. They are so logical; they expect to see "M**y** **c**at **i**s **cu**te." to be "M**i k**at **i**z **qu**t." When words are thrown randomly at people to read, young children who can only learn logically feel the problem with the way English is written but are too young to diagnose the problem. They are not trained linguists and are too young to form all the linguistic questions they wish to ask. If the IBIA is not applied, logical learners will have difficulties in reading or spelling or in both.

Step 6 Avoid using other books that introduce more than one spelling pattern at a time, because that would be like introducing 180 people standing in a queue and then expecting people to remember all of their names. For instance, before asking students to read any words that contain the "**sh**" phonic as in "fi**sh**," you may inform them and then show them how the letter "**s**" combined with the letter "**h**" produce the single sound of "**sh**." You may also justify the use of the "**sh**" by informing them that because English did not have a single letter to represent the sound of "**sh**" the two letters "**s+h**" were combined to represent this sound.

Step 7 The grouping of words of a same sound and spelling pattern is prepared for you in each lesson; simply teach the same words grouped in each lesson.

Step 8 In *Read Instantly*, learners are constantly informed about a change that is about to occur before asking them to read any words that contain such changes. The following examples demonstrate how letters can make sounds different from their letter names, and students need to be gradually informed before introducing each such change:

1. The "h" sound as in "hot" differs from its sound in "th" as in "mouth."

2. The "s" sound as in "rose" and "has" sounds like a "z."

3. The "g" sounds like its letter name in "huge," but not in "hug."

4. The "a" sounds like its letter name in "main," but not in "man" and not in "auto."

5. The "e" sounds like its letter name in "meat," but not in "met" and not in "trailer."

6. The "i" sounds like its letter name in "hide," but not in "hid" and not in "skirt."

7. The "o" sounds like its letter name in "hope," but not in "hop" and not in "choir."

8. The "u" sounds like its letter name in "mute," but not in "mutt" and not in "virus."

9. The "c" sounds like its letter name in "cell," like the "k" in "cup," like the "sh" in "social," and like the name of the letter "q" in "cute."

10. The "q" always sounds like the letter "k," not like the name of the letter "q" and every "q" is followed by a "u"—students must be informed ahead of time that every "q" is followed by a "u." They also need to be informed that every "qu" is followed by a vowel and that the "qu" sounds like "kw" as in "quit." The sound of the actual letter "q" is not found in "q," but in "cu" as in cute, cucumber, accumulate, cure, secure, etc.

11. After informing learners that a letter's name can differ from its sound when used in words, inform them that a single sound can be written in several ways (many spelling patterns). For instance, this final sound in these words is spelled in seven different ways, as in fashion, ocean, suspicion, complexion, superstition, expression, and musician. If such endings are presented too soon, they can cause a learner to veer away from learning. A learner may think something is wrong with his or her ability to learn.

12. There are 26 English letters and 13 of these letters change and make sounds that are different from their letter names; it makes no sense to tell learners that the name of this letter is "c" as in "cat" before informing them that the "c" can sound like a "k." Otherwise, they may read "cat" as "sat."

13. This examples show the changes in the sounds and spelling patterns of the vowel "a" alone: [ā: rain, ate, day, able] [ă: fat, fatter] [ə: permanent] [ɔ: fall, false, auto, law] [a: war]

Step 9 Planned Lessons: The steps in which phonics are introduced in *Read Instantly* are not random; lessons are carefully planned and no new letter, sound or spelling pattern is introduced without a warning of its changes beforehand. Hence, anyone capable of learning the alphabet, including dyslexic persons can immediately read from this book. They continue to read aloud without a stop, until all the different spelling patterns of all the English sounds are memorized.

Step 10 Read the direct instructions before each lesson and explain that to students. In the beginning, avoid asking students to read any words that contain ✓Hard c ✓Hard g ✓The "s" that sounds like a "z" as in "was" ✓Double letters as in "add" ✓The "y" as a vowel as in "gym" ✓Consonant blends like "st" in "stamp" ✓Digraphs like the "sh" in "ship" ✓Two vowels in a word like "**ea**" in "m**ea**t" ✓Silent letters like "***k***" in "***k***not" ✓Words endings like "**tion**" in "ac**tion**" ✓Long words ✓Begin with words that contain one vowel as presented at in this book.

Step 11 Disallow speed-reading before learning to read and spell. Forced speed-reading before learning to read and spell words causes learners to see letters in reverse and then spelling them in reverse. Dyslexia in spelling and in writing letters in reverse ends, after learning to spell and after slowing down to write words slowly.

Step 12 Insist on students reading aloud. Explain to students, from the first day of class, that we acquire information through our five senses and show them how that works. Continue to insist until they read all the practice lessons aloud, whether in or outside of the classroom. If in a classroom, they need to read aloud together in one rhythm. Read more on page 53.

Step 13 Vowels rule English and they cannot be avoided. Explain that to students and ask them to focus their vision on the vowels when they read. Inform them that learning all the 38 sounds and 96 spelling patterns of vowel is the most important part of learning to read and spell.

Step 14 Warn students that 13 of the 26 letters will be making sounds that are different from their letter names; especially, the five vowels and eight inconsistent consonants. The eight consonants have 50 sounds that are spelled in 60 spelling patterns.

Step 15 Do not force learning and do not stop too long to memorize the spelling of every single word. Learning to spell will be acquired naturally as students keep reading aloud slowly. More spelling rules with detailed practice lessons are in *Learn to Spell 500 Words a Day*, wherein each vowel is isolated in a book.

Step 16 The first four chapters in *Read Instantly* may seem easy for some learners, but Chapters 5 to 9 become gradually sophisticated as each vowel is dissected and isolated in a chapter.

Step 17 Explain all the symbols and concepts used in this book gradually and as needed. For instance, *Italic letters* in this book represent silent letters, like the silent ***p*** in recei***p***t. However, students do not need to know that until they reach Lesson 6 in Chapter 1 wherein silent letters are introduced.

Step 18 Before asking students to write, ask them to read this entire book aloud slowly. Students must learn to read first before they can begin to write. The steps of language acquisition are speaking, reading, and then writing.

Step 19 When your students finish reading this entire book fluently, they will understand the way English words are structured and will apply their learning to any other words they see.

Step 20 After reading this book fluently, students will do well in schools but will need to learn more words from the rest of the books by Camilia Sadik. In this book for instance, the **ea** phonic as in m**ea**t is presented in 48 words, while all 370 **ea** words are presented in the *Vowel E* book.

More about *Read Instantly*

Comprehensive Phonics: Unlike most books that teach bits and pieces of phonics, *Read Instantly* is a comprehensive book of phonics. Its 200 phonics lessons cover over 180 spelling patterns of more than 90 sounds we call phonics. In it lies the foundation for learning the rules that govern the reading and spelling of phonics.

Beginners are Children or Adults: This specific textbook or workbook is for beginners who have not yet learned phonics, or for those who missed learning phonics when they were growing up. Beginners may be any age and can be those who cannot yet read any words, or those who can read but cannot spell the words that they read. This book is for all ages and all types of learners.

Logical Learning Style: Children and adults with spelling difficulties need to start with *Read Instantly* to learn the basic rules that govern phonics, even if they can read and comprehend. Learners with spelling difficulties learn differently; their learning style is a logical learning style. They need logical spelling rules before they can memorize the spelling of words.

Who is this book for?

The book *Read Instantly* has been successfully used by:

a. parents to teach reading before sending children to school,

b. homeschooling parents of K-12 to teach reading and spelling,

c. teachers as a resource book to teach reading phonics in K-3,

d. community college teachers, adult school teachers, and tutors at adult literacy centers,

e. ESL teachers to teach reading phonics to international students,

f. dyslexic person to learn to read or spell or both,

g. high school dropouts were helped by tutors,

h. adult English speakers as a self-help book for learning to spell,

i. and countless brain-injured students who learned to read and spell instantly from it. Apparently, brain-injured persons become logical learners, the book was not intentionally written for them, but it has been successfully working for them.

Read Instantly has been helping those who everyone else has given up on them.

1 Short Vowels, Double Consonants, Silent Letters, Consonant Blends

Chapter 1: Short Vowels

"M**y** **c**at i**s** **cu**te." vs. "M**i** **k**at i**z** **qu**t."?

Lesson 1: Read the **names** of the 26 English letters

Read aloud as many times as needed until you have memorized the names of the 26 letters. The five basic vowels are **a, e, i, o,** and **u**; and the consonants are the rest of the letters. Memorize the names of the five basic vowels in the same order they are written. Vowels are more important than the consonants—primarily because each vowel produces many different sounds while consonants are silent, unless they are paired with a vowel. Vowels are responsible for the sounds we make in our speech. Learning all the sounds and spelling patterns of each vowel is the most important part of learning to read and spell. Vowels rule English and they cannot be avoided.

If you need to learn the names of the English letters, read them aloud as many times as needed until you memorize them:

a   b   c   d   e   f   g

h   i   j   k   l   m   n

o   p   q   r   s   t   u

v   w   x   y   z

Memorize the five basic vowels in the same order they are written:

a   e   i   o   u

5

Lesson 2: Read the first **sound** of each letter

There is a difference between a letter's name and its sound when used in words. Half of the 26 English letters make sounds that differ from their letter names. Because the "q" does not sound like its letter name, it is being placed in a queue awaiting its turn to be introduced as a letter that sounds like a "k." Read the first **sound** that each English letter makes, except the "q":

a at	b bat	c cell
d dot	e set	f fit
g gel	h hat	i it
j job	k kit	l lip
m man	n nap	o hot
p pen	r ran	s sat
t ten	u up	v vet
w win	x fax	y yes
z zip		

Teaching Instructions

❌ For now, all the spelling patterns of phonics are placed in a queue. Follow the order of the lessons introduced in this book, and <mark>avoid</mark> teaching any words that contain:

❌ The hard **c**

❌ The hard **g**

❌ The **qu**

❌ The "**s**" that sounds like a "**z**" as in "i**s**"

❌ Double letters as in "a**dd**"

❌ The "**y**" as a vowel as in "m**y**"

❌ Consonant blends as in "**str**ong"

❌ Digraphs of "**h**" as in "fi**sh**"

❌ Two vowels in a word as in "b**oa**t"

❌ Any long multi-syllabic words

❌ Any words with suffixes as in "mathemati**cian**"

❌ Any words with prefixes as in "**un**happy"

✅ Simply follow the order of lessons introduced, and then presented in this book. For now, all the spelling patterns of the sounds we call phonics are <mark>placed in a queue</mark> awaiting their turn to be introduced logically, one-at-a-time, and then presented in a number of words.

Notice that so far, no consonant different from its letter name has been introduced, and from now onward, you will notice that each sound is introduced and explained before presenting it. If your students are not able to read, please explain the justifications or rules before each lesson and then ask them to read the words in that practice lesson aloud.

✅ **Explain** to students that it is not enough to learn the 26 letters and that they will need to learn phonics too. The 26 letters produce over 90 sounds we call phonics that are spelled in many different spelling patterns. Examples of phonics are the "**au**" in "l**au**ndry," the "**cian**" in "mathemati**cian**," and the "**y**" in "m**y**."

We need not expect a new learner who has just learned the ABC's to read a sentence like "M**y c**at i**s cu**te." because that new learner, especially if his or her learning style is a logical learning style expect to see "M**y c**at i**s cu**te" to be "Mi kat is qut." More than half of the population has a logical learning style and therefore needs logic before it can memorize. To insure that all types of learners will learn to read and spell, we need to apply the principle of **I**nforming **B**efore **I**ntroducing, which is applied throughout this entire book. In this specific case, we need to inform learners beforehand that the "y" can sound like an "i" at the end of short one-syllable words as in "my, sky, try, etc."; the "c" can sound like a "k" as in "cat"; the "s" can sound like a "z" at the end of short one-syllable words as in "is, was, has, etc."; and that the sound of the name of the letter "q" is not found in "q" but in "cu" as in "cute, cure, cucumber, occupy, etc."

Lesson 3: Learn the short vowels in 180 words:

ă ě ĭ ŏ ŭ

Each vowel has this unique short sound. Read these words aloud as many times as needed until fluency is achieved. Focus on the unique **short ă** sound in these words:

at	sat	fat	rat
mat	Nat	hat	vat
pat	man	ran	van
fan	tan	ban	pan
Dan	Jan	map	nap
lap	tap	zap	sap
pap	yap	hap	Sam
Pam	jam	dam	ram
yam	am	mad	bad
pad	sad	had	fad
dad	lad	ad	Al
pal	tab	lab	dab
jab	nab	wax	tax
fax	ax	Max	

Continue to read aloud and focus on the unique **short ĕ** sound:

set	met	pet	wet
bet	vet	net	yet
let	jet	bed	red
fed	wed	led	med
Ned	Ted	Ed	men
pen	ten	den	fen
hen	yen	Ben	Ken
web	Deb	pep	hex

Continue to read aloud and focus on the unique **short ĭ** sound:

sit	bit	kit	hit
pit	lit	it	Tim
Jim	Kim	rim	him
dim	vim	fib	bib
lib	rib	nib	hip
sip	lip	tip	six
fix	mix	sin	bin
fin	win	kin	din

Read Instantly by Camilia Sadik

tin	pin	in		lid
hid	did	bid		

Continue to read aloud and focus on the unique **short ŏ** sound:

Tom	mom		Bob	mob
rob	Rob	job		sob
fob		box	fox		top
hop	mop		not	hot
pot	dot	lot		jot
Ron	on	non		rod
sod	nod	pod		

Continue to read aloud and focus on the unique **short ŭ** sound:

us	bus		fun	run
sun	bun	pun		nun
up	pup		tub	sub
rub	hub	pub		dub
but	nut	hut		rum
bum	hum	sum		Bud
bud	dud	mud		

Chapter 1: Short Vowels

This is a one-page list of the same above 180 words that contain **short vowels**:

at   sat   fat   rat   mat   Nat   hat   at   pat   man   ran   van
fan   tan   ban   pan   Dan   Jan   map   nap   lap   tap   zap   sap
pap   yap   hap   Sam   Pam   jam   dam   ram   yam   am   mad   bad
pad   sad   had   fad   dad   lad   ad   Al   pal   tab   lab   dab
jab   nab   wax   tax   fax   ax   Max

set   met   pet   wet   bet   vet   net   yet   let   jet   bed   red
fed   wed   led   med   Ned   Ted   Ed   men   pen   ten   den   fen
hen   yen   Ben   Ken   web   Deb   pep   hex   vex

sit   bit   kit   hit   pit   lit   it   Tim   Jim   Kim   rim   him
dim   vim   fib   lib   rib   nib   bib   hip   sip   lip   tip   six
fix   mix   sin   bin   fin   win   kin   din   tin   pin   in   lid
hid   did   bid

Tom   mom   Bob   mob   rob   Rob   job   sob   fob   box   fox   top
hop   mop   not   hot   pot   dot   lot   jot   Ron   on   non   rod
sod   nod   pod

us   bus   fun   run   sun   bun   pun   nun   up   pup   tub   sub
rub   hub   pub   dub   but   nut   hut   Bud   bud   dud   mud   bum
hum   sum   rum

Lesson 4: There are double letters in English, as in "i**nn**."

Inform that sometimes consonants double for many different reasons that will be explained later. For instance, the "**n**" doubles in "i**nn**" to tell it apart from "i**n**," and the "**d**" doubles in "a**dd**" to differentiate it from "a**d**."

Read aloud and focus on the double letters in these words:

| i**nn** | a**dd** | mi**tt** | mu**tt** | o**dd** | To**dd** |

Lesson 5: The **ss, ff, ll, zz** come in doubles at the end of short words

Inform students that the **ss, ff, ll, and zz often come in doubles** at the end of short words that contain one vowel. Justify by explaining to students that the one "s" is so weak that its sound can turn into a "z" sound as in "ha**s**, wa**s**, bag**s**, etc."; therefore, we often have to double the "s."

Read aloud and focus on the double letters at the end of these words:

pa**ss**	ma**ss**	ba**ss**	le**ss**
me**ss**	ki**ss**	mi**ss**	bo**ss**
to**ss**	Je**ff**	mi**ff**	pu**ff**
bu**ff**	mu**ff**	ru**ff**	te**ll**
se**ll**	ce**ll**	be**ll**	ye**ll**
he**ll**	fe**ll**	we**ll**	i**ll**
hi**ll**	pi**ll**	bi**ll**	di**ll**
wi**ll**	fi**ll**	si**ll**	mi**ll**
ja**zz**	fu**zz**	bu**zz**	

Lesson 6: There are silent letters in English, as in "bom*b*"

Inform that some letters are silent for many different reasons, which will be explained later. For instance, the silent "*k*" in "*k*not" is useful to tell apart two words like "not" and "*k*not." Remember that italic fonts represent silent letters in this book.

Read aloud and focus on the silent letters that are *italicized*:

    *k*not   *k*nob   *k*nit   lo*dg*e

    dum*b*   bom*b*

Lesson 7: Introducing the consonant blends, as in "**dr**ess"

Inform students that consonant blends are two or three consonants next to each other with **no vowel** between them, like the "**str**" in "**str**ong." Meanwhile, continue to avoid presenting any words that contain hard **c**, hard **g**, **qu**, the **s** like **z** (ha**s**), the **y** as a vowel (g**y**m), digraphs (**sh**ip), two vowels in a word (t**ie**), any long words, any words endings (**tion**), and simply adhere to the order of words listed in this book's lessons.

Read aloud if you need to learn the consonant blends at the **beginning** of words:

bled	**bl**ess	**dr**ess	**dr**op
dwell	**br**an	**fl**at	**fl**ed
Fred	**pl**an	**pl**ot	**pr**ess
stop	**st**ep	**sl**im	**sl**am
smell	**sp**ill	**sp**ell	**sk**ip
snap	**sn**iff	**sw**am	**sw**ell
stub	**st**uff	**tr**ip	**tr**ap
strap	**str**ess	**tw**in	**spr**int

Read Instantly by Camilia Sadik

Read aloud if you need to learn the consonant blends at the **end** of words:

lamp	jump	bank	sink
mask	desk	help	milk
felt	lift	kept	wept
bend	bent	best	farm
park	perk	surf	harp
tarp	burp	mart	art
next	text	stamp	slept
blend	end		

Bravo! You just read over 290 words!

Lesson 8: Compare the five short vowels in 171 essential words

Compare these very important words that will form components of thousands of long words in the future. Read aloud slowly as many times as needed until you achieve fluency. Focus your vision on the vowels when you read:

Compare the short vowels' sounds in these very important words:

Short ă	Short ĕ	Short ĭ	Short ŏ	Short ŭ
mad	med	mid	mod	mud
pap	pep	pip	pop	pup
hat		hit	hot	hut
Dan	den	din	Don	dun
mass	mess	miss	moss	muss
an		in	on	un
fan	fen	fin		fun
pan	pen	pin		pun
bad	bed	bid		bud
Hal	hell	hill		hull
ban	Ben	bin		bun
dam		dim		dumb
add	Ed		odd	
sad		Sid	sod	
dad		did		dud
tap		tip	top	
slam		slim		slum
sap		sip	sop	
hap		hip	hop	
bass			boss	bus

sax		six	sox
fax		fix	fox
at		it	
had		hid	
fad	fed		
pad			pod
map			mop
lap		lip	
zap		zip	
tab				tub
jab			job
stab				stub
ran			Ron	run
man	men		
tan	ten	tin	
pal		pill	
Sal	sell	sill	
Al		ill	
Sam				sum
lap		lip	
	step		stop
slap		slip	
	red	rid	rod
	let	lit	lot
	led	lid	

jet		jot	
wet	wit		
Ted		Todd	
Ned		nod	
	rib	rob	rub
	nib	knob	nub
	bib	Bob	
		sob	sub
	sin		sun
	win	won	
		non	nun
bell	bill	boll	
fell	fill		
well	will		
	him		hum
	Tim	Tom	
		bomb	bum
	fizz		fuzz

17

Teaching Instructions

The rest of the spelling patterns of the sounds we call phonics are placed in a **queue** awaiting their turn to be introduced logically, one-at-a-time, and then presented in a number of words. **I**nform **B**efore **I**ntroducing each new phonic throughout your use of this entire book. Begin by explaining the meanings of some of the symbols and concepts used in this book.

✗ Now is the time to warn students that each vowel can make many sounds that are different from its letter name. Each vowel and its changes are presented in a separate chapter in the second half of this book. Introduce and explain these examples of some of the changes in each vowel: m**e**t, m**ea**t; m**a**n, m**ai**n; r**o**d, r**oa**d

✗ Continue to avoid teaching any words that contain:
Hard **c**, hard **g**, **qu**, **s** like **z** (ha**s**), **y** like a vowel (g**y**m), digraphs (**sh**ip), two vowels in a word (m**ee**t), long words, words with suffixes (**tion**), words with prefixes (**ac**), and simply follow the order of words in the lessons presented in this book.

✓ Explain that **dots** inside words represent a division of words into **syllables** as in "win·dow." A syllable is a part of a word, which contains one vowel sound. There are two syllables in "win·dow," "win" and "dow." There are two syllables in "o·pen," "o" and "pen." There is only one syllable in "me." There are three syllables in "me·di·a." There are two syllables in "vow·el," "vow" and "el." Explain that long words are made of smaller parts called syllables.

✓ Inform before the next lesson and repeat the following points to students:

- The five vowels are a, e, i, o, and u and wait for introducing the "y" and the "w" as vowels. Explain that vowels often help each other like the "a" helping the "e" in "meat" by making it sound long like the name of the letter "E."
- In this book, **dots** inside words indicate a division of a word into syllables, as in "win·dow."
- A **syllable** is a part of a word that contains one vowel sound, as in "con·tin·ue."
- A **stressed syllable** in a word is the one that is said with more stress, as in "a´·ble."
- The **short vowels'** symbols are: ă, ĕ, ĭ, ŏ, ŭ
- Each of the short vowels has one special unique sound.
- The **long vowels'** symbols are: ā, ē, ī, ō, ū
- The long ā sounds like the **name** of the letter **A** as in r**ai**n.
- The long ē sounds like the **name** of the letter **E** as in m**ea**t.
- The long ī sounds like the **name** of the letter **I** as in t**ie**.
- The long ō sounds like the **name** of the letter **O** as in b**oa**t.
- The long ū sounds like the **name** of the letter **U** as in contin**ue**.

2 Introduction to Long Vowels and Two Vowels Spelling Rules

  ī ō
ă ĕ ĭ ŏ ŭ

 Lesson 1: Two vowels walking Rule: āi in rain, ēa in meat, īe in tie, ōa in boat, ūe in blue

āi Rule "**When two vowels are walking, the first one does the talking.**" This rule means that as in "rain," when the two vowels "a" and "i" are next to each other (walking) in a syllable that is stressed, the first one "a" does the talking by saying its letter name **A** (ay), and the second one "i" is silent.

 Read aloud slowly the words in each practice lesson whether asked or not asked to do so:

main	rain	brain	pain
lain	plain	vain	stain
mail	sail	pail	fail
hail	tail	nail	bait
wait	maid	raid	braid
aid	aim	paint	faint

 Compare the short ă with the long ā in these words:

man, main	ran, rain	bran, brain
pan, pain	van, vain	plan, plain
mad, maid	brad, braid	pad, paid
am, aim	bat, bait	pal, pail

Two vowels walking Rule (ēa in meat)

ēa Rule As in "meat," when the two vowels "e" and "a" are walking in a stressed syllable, the first vowel "e" does the talking by saying its letter name **E**, and the second vowel "a" is silent. Read these words aloud slowly and always focus your vision on the vowels:

meat	eat	seat	neat
heat	feat	bead	lead
flea	bean	mean	dean
seal	heal	dream	team
tea	sea	weak	wean

Compare the short ĕ with the long ē in these words:

met, meat	set, seat	net, neat
men, mean	hell, heal	sell, seal
bed, bead	red, read	led, lead

Two vowels walking Rule (īe in tie)

īe Rule As in "tie," when the two vowels "i" and "e" are walking in a stressed syllable, the first vowel "i" does the talking by saying its letter name **I** and the second vowel "e" is silent. Read these words aloud slowly and focus your vision on the vowels:

| tie | tied | die | died |
| lie | lied | pie | pies |

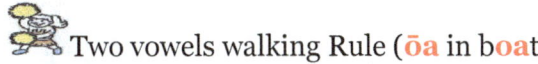

Two vowels walking Rule (ōa in boat)

ōa Rule As in "road," when the two vowels "o" and "a" are walking in a stressed syllable, the first vowel "o" does the talking by saying its letter name **O** (oh) and the second vowel "*a*" is silent.

Read aloud slowly whether alone or in a class:

boat	oat	float	road
toad	load	loan	Joan
foam	soap	soak	toast
roast	boast	loaf	soar

Compare the short ŏ with the long ō in these words:

Todd, toad   rod, road   toss, toast

The two vowels walking Rule (ūe in blue)

ūe Rule As in "blue," when the two vowels "u" and "e" are walking in a stressed syllable, the first vowel "u" does the talking by saying its letter name **U** (you) and the second vowel "*e*" is silent."

| blue | flue | due | true |
| sue | hue | | |

Read Instantly by Camilia Sadik

Lesson 2: The *a-e* can still walk Rule: fāte, Pēte, bīte, hōpe, tūbe

ā-i Rule Compare "fat" with "fate." One consonant between two vowels is too weak to keep the two vowels from walking. As in "fate," the two vowels "a-e" can still help one another when there is only one consonant like the one "t" between them. The first vowel "a" does the talking, while the second vowel "e" is silent. This explains the reason consonants double as in (fat→fatter→fattest); it is because one consonant "t" between two vowels is too **weak** to keep the two vowels from walking together. This is especially true when the "e" is silent at the end of a syllable.

Read aloud slowly whether or not you are asked to do so:

hate	fate	rate	mate
ate	fade	tape	same
plane	pale	male	ale
made	Jake	make	take
lake	wave	Dave	save

Compare short ă with long ā in these words:

fat, fate	hat, hate	rat, rate
mat, mate	at, ate	fad, fade
mad, made	Sam, same	mal, male
pal, pale	plan, plane	tap, tape

The **i-e** can still walk Rule (ī-e in bīte)

ī-e Rule Compare "b**i**t" with "b**i**t**e**." As in "b**it****e**," the silent "**e**" can reach through the one "**t**" and help the "**i**" sound like the name of the letter **I**, and the reason is that one consonant "**t**" between the two vowels (**i-e**) is too **weak** to keep the two vowels from walking together:

b**it***e*	k**it***e*	s**it***e*	sp**it***e*
b**id***e*	h**id***e*	s**id***e*	r**id***e*
d**im***e*	t**im***e*	r**im***e*	sl**im***e*
T**im***e*	d**in***e*	f**in***e*	m**in***e*
l**in***e*	b**ik***e*	l**ik***e*	h**ik***e*

Compare the short ĭ with the long ī in these words:

b**i**t, b**it***e*	b**i**d, b**id***e*	h**i**d, h**id***e*
k**i**t, k**it***e*	s**i**t, s**it***e*	d**i**m, d**im***e*
sl**i**m, sl**im***e*	r**i**m, r**im***e*	T**i**m, T**im***e*

23

Read Instantly by Camilia Sadik

The **o-e** can still walk Rule (ō-e in hōpe)

ō-e Rule Compare "hop" with "hope." As in "hope," the silent "*e*" can reach through the one "**p**" and help the "**o**" sound like the name of the letter **O** (oh), and the reason is that one consonant "**p**" between the two vowels (o-e) is too **weak** to keep the two vowels from walking together:

note	dote	re·mote	vote
hope	mope	robe	ode
bone	stone	dole	sole
hole	pope	slope	joke

Compare the short ŏ with the long ō in these words:

rob, robe   not, note   dot, dote

pop, pope   hop, hope   mop, mope

slop, slope   odd, ode

24

The e-e can still walk Rule (ē-e in Pēte)

ē-e Rule Compare "met" with "mete." As in "mete," the final silent "*e*" can reach through the one "**t**" and help the first "*e*" sound like the name of the letter **E** (ee), and the reason is that one consonant "**t**" between the two vowels (e-e) is too **weak** to keep the two vowels from walking together.

mete	Pete	here	mere
sin·cere	gene	re·cede	eve
Eve	Steve	Le·ba·nese	eke

Compare the short ĕ with the long ē in these words:

met, mete   pet, Pete

The u-e can still walking Rule (ū-e in tūbe)

ū-e Rule Compare "tub" with "tube." As in "tube," the silent "*e*" can reach through the one "**b**" and help the "**u**" sound like the name of the letter **U** (you), and the reason is that one consonant "**b**" between the two vowels (u-e) is too **weak** to keep the two vowels from walking together:

tube	mute	jute	flute
rule	mule	fume	per·fume
huge	re·fuge	truce	re·duce

Compare the short ŭ with the long ū in these words:

tub, tube   mutt, mute

Bravo! You just read 156 new words!

Teaching Instructions

✓ **You may now teach:**
✓ You may now teach any double consonants.
✓ You may now teach any consonant blends.

✗ For the next chapter, please continue to **avoid** teaching any words that contain:
✗ Hard **c**
✗ Hard **g**
✗ The **qu**
✗ The "**s**" that sounds like "**z**" as in "wa**s**"
✗ The "**y**" as a vowel as in "sk**y**"
✗ Digraphs of "h" as in "fi**sh**"
✗ Double vowels in one syllable as in "b**oo**k"
✗ Any long multi-syllabic words
✗ Any words with suffixes as in "na**tion**"
✗ Any words with prefixes as in "**un**happy"

Simply adhere to the order of lessons introduced then presented in this book. For now, the rest of the spelling patterns of phonics are placed in a **queue** awaiting their turn to be introduced logically, one-at-a-time, and then presented in a number of words.

Notice that so far, no consonant different from its letter name has been introduced, and from now on, you will notice that each sound is introduced and explained before presenting it. If your students are not able to read, please explain the justifications or rules before each lesson and then ask them to read the words aloud.

3 Inconsistent Consonants: y, h, c, g, q, x, s, ve, ac

y h c g q x s ve ac

Lesson 1: The consonant "**y**" as a vowel: m**y**, cit**y**, d**ay**, b**oy**, g**y**m

As in "**yes**," the "**y**" at the beginning of words is a consonant, but it changes to a long vowel when it falls at the **end** of a word or at the end of a syllable. Usually, the final "**y**" sounds like long **ī** in short one-syllable words as in "sk**y**," like long **ē** in long more than one syllable words as in "histor**y**," like long **ā** in "**āy**" as in "d**ay**," like long **ō** in "**ōy**" as in "b**oy**," and like a shot **ĭ** in the middle of words or syllables as in "g**y**m."

y says i Read aloud the "y" like the long **ī** at the end of short, mainly one-syllable words:

m**y**	sk**y**	sp**y**	sl**y**
tr**y**	dr**y**	fr**y**	fr**y**·er
pr**y**	pl**y**	b**y**	b**u**y

y says e Read the "y" like the long **ē** at the end of long words that have more than one syllable:

cit·**y**	par·t**y**	hap·p**y**	wind·**y**
fuss·**y**	fun·n**y**	fan·c**y**	sad·l**y**
bad·l**y**	mar·r**y**	em*p*·t**y**	his·to·r**y**

ay says a Read aloud the "ay" like the long **ā** sound:

d**ay**	r**ay**	R**ay**	pr**ay**
tr**ay**	w**ay**	l**ay**	pl**ay**
p**ay**	s**ay**	st**ay**	o·k**ay**
m**ay**	to·d**ay**	j**ay**	b**ay**

27

oy says ōy Read aloud the "oy" like "ōy":

    b**oy**   t**oy**   j**oy**   en·j**oy**

    em·pl**oy**   em·pl**oy**·ment

y says ĭ Read aloud the "y" like the short vowel ĭ when in the middle of syllables:

    g**y**m   L**y**nn   c**y**st   h**y**m*n*

Compare these words:

    m**y**, m**a**y   pr**y**, pr**a**y   pl**y**, pl**a**y

    fr**y**, fr**a**y   re·pl**y**, re·pl**a**y   sl**y**, sl**a**y

Bravo! You just read 62 new words.

You MUST read aloud slowly in order to memorize.

If learners are in a classroom, the entire class may read aloud slowly together in one rhythm. Beginners need to read slowly to see the way words are spelled. To avoid seeing letters and words in reverse, beginners need to read slowly. To prevent dyslexia, learners must not speed-read before learning to read and spell.

Lesson 2: The **11** digraphs of **H**: **sh**ip, **th**is, **th**ink, ea**ch**, s**ch**ool, **ch**ef, **ph**oto, **wh**o, **wh**en, ri**gh**t, tou**gh**

H The following 11 sounds are produced by specific letters sticking to the letter "**h**" to produce a single **new** sound. For instance, the "**sh**" in "**sh**ip" is a single sound. The "**sh**" is needed because there is no single English letter to represent this sound. These **11** new sounds produced by the "**h**" and another letter are called "digraphs" and each one of them is considered a phonic.

Phonics: As in the "**sh**" in "**sh**ip," the "**tion**" in "na**tion**," and the "**au**" in "**au**ction," a phonic is a single sound produced by a letter that does not sound like its name or by a combination of two or more letters. Each phonic acts like an additional letter that could theoretically be added to the English alphabet. 👉 If in a classroom, the entire class needs to read aloud slowly together and in one rhythm:

sh

ship	**sh**ift	**sh**op	**sh**ot
shell	**sh**irt	**sh**ark	**sh**ut
fi**sh**	wa**sh**	ma**sh**	a**sh**
ra**sh**	ru**sh**	fre**sh**	mar·**sh**al
a**sh**·tray	a·**sh**am*e*d		

soft th

this	**th**at	**th**e	fa·**th**er
mo**th**·er	o**th**·er		

hard th

ba**th**	bir**th**	**th**ink	**th**rob
thum*b*	**th**un·der		

Soft ch

    chin   chips   chop   chat

    chess   much   butch·er   cheers

ch says k

    school   Chris   ache   tech

    scheme

ch says sh

    chef   ma·chine   cha·let   mous·tache

    par·a·chute

ph says f

    phone   pho·to   phar·ma·cy

wh says h

    who   who·ever   whom   whose

    whole   whole·sale

wh says w or hw

when   whenever   why   what
where   whether

gh says f

enough   tough   rough

silent gh

high   higher   highest   highly
highway   highlight   thigh   light
right   bright   night   knight

You read 82 new words.

×Avoid

× Continue to avoid teaching any words that contain hard **c**, hard **g**, **qu**, **s** like **z** (i**s**), some two vowels in a syllable (**su**it), most long words, words with suffixes (**tion**), words with prefixes (**ac**), and simply adhere to the order of lessons presented in this book.

Read Instantly by Camilia Sadik

Lesson 3: The soft and the hard **C** sounds

The **soft** "**c**" sounds like the name of the letter "**c**" as in "**c**ity," but the hard "**c**" sounds like the "**k**" as in "**c**at." The "**c**" is soft when followed by **e**, **i**, or **y**. However, the "**c**" is hard like a "**k**" when followed by **a**, **o**, **u**, a consonant, and when it is not followed by anything as in "fantasti**c**."

ce, ci, cy

 Read the "**c**" like the name of the letter **C** when followed by **e**, **i**, or **y** as in:

ce

cell	cent	face
ace	rice	price
ice	since	li·cense

ci

ci·ty	cin·e·ma	so·ci·e·ty
de·cide	phar·ma·cist	cit·i·zen
cit·i·zen·ship		

cy

phar·ma·cy	mer·cy	fan·cy
Nan·cy	Sta·cy	pol·i·cy
lit·er·a·cy	cyst	Cy·prus
Cyn·thi·a	cy·ber	cy·press

32

Hard C

The letter "**k**" is limited in its use and it is not allowed in long words; thus, we need the hard "**c**" to represent the sound of "**k**" in long words and in most words. Read the "**c**" like "**k**" when followed by **a**, **o**, **u**, or by a consonant, and when not followed by anything as in "magi**c**." In addition, read the "**c**" like "**k**" when preceded by a vowel in the same syllable like the "**ac**" in "**ac**·ci·dent," "**ec**" in "d**ec**k," "**ic**" in "s**ic**k," "**oc**" in "**oc**·cur," "**uc**" in "l**uc**k," and as in the following examples:

Hard C
ca, co, cu, cl, cr, ct, ch, ac, ec, ic, oc, uc

ca says ka

cat	**ca**r	**ca**rt
card	**ca**n	**ca**ke
ca·reer	**ca**b	**ca**m·er·a
can·dy	a·**ca**d·e·my	mag·i·**ca**l
s**ca**b	s**ca**n	s**ca**n·dal

co says ko

cop	**co**pe	**co**t
cot·ton	**co**w	**co**ld
core	s**co**re	**co**n·so·nant

33

cu says ku

cut	cute	cuffs
cus·tard	cir·cus	cult
scum	cup	cup·board

cl says kl

clip	clap	class
club	cliff	ac·cli·mate
clean	claim	ac·claim
pro·claim	clear	cli·ché
de·cline	in·cline	re·clin·er
clone	con·clude	in·clude
in·clud·ed	ex·clude	

cr says kr

craft	crib	crust
cross	cream	screen
scroll	cry	scrub
con·crete	de·scribe	ac·ro·bat

ct says kt

act	re·act	fact
ac·tor	con·tact	prac·tice
pact	im·pact	tract
at·tract	tact	vic·to·ry
prac·ti·cal	doc·tor	Oc·to·ber

ch says k

chem·is·try	char·ac·ter	tech·ni·cal
ache	al·che·my	scheme
or·ches·tra	ar·chi·tect	or·chid
ar·chives	chi·ro·prac·tor	ech·o
psy·chi·a·try	schiz·o·phre·ni·a	cat·e·chism
mas·o·chist	Ar·chi·me·des	an·ar·chy
mon·ar·chy	hi·er·ar·chy	head·ache
me·chan·i·cal	scho·las·tic	cha·o·tic
chron·ic	chron·o·log·i·cal	ar·cha·ic
stom·ach·ache	back·ache	cho·les·terol
chol·e·ra	psy·chol·o·gy	

ac says ak

ac·cept	ac·cent	ac·cess
ac·claim	ac·cede	ac·com·plish
ac·ci·dent	Mac	Jack
back	pack	back·pack
pack·et	rack	crack
lack	black	slacks
whack	whacked	

ec says ek

deck	neck	peck
wreck	wrecked	wreck·age

oc says ok

oc·cur	oc·cu·py	lock
block	clock	mock
knock	rock	sock
dock	stock	stocked

Chapter 3: y, h, c, g, q, x, s, ve, ac

ic says ik

fan·tas·t**ic**	plas·t**ic**	mag·**ic**
ba·s**ic**	phon·**ic**	Ar·a·b**ic**
Ar·a·ma·**ic**	clin·**ic**	ar·tis·t**ic**
Soc·ra·t**ic**	skep·t**ic**	sar·cas·t**ic**
sur·re·al·is·t**ic**	ec·o·nom·**ic**	me·chan·**ic**
chron·**ic**	i·tal·**ic**	traf·f**ic**
lyr·**ic**	s**ick**	t**ick**
th**ick**	cl**ick**	sl**ick**
p**ick**	k**ick**	N**ick**

uc says uk

l**uck**	l**uck**·y	d**uck**
b**uck**	b**uck**·et	t**uck**
tr**uck**	st**uck**	str**uck**

✗ Continue to avoid teaching any words that contain hard **g**, **qu**, **s** like **z** (ha**s**), some two vowels in a word (h**ea**d), most long words, words with suffixes (**tion**), words with prefixes (**un**), and simply stick with the order of lessons presented in this book.

Read Instantly by Camilia Sadik

Lesson 4: The soft and hard **G** sounds

As in "lar**g**e," the **soft** "**g**" sounds like the name of the letter **G**, and the hard "**g**" sounds like the "**g**" as in "**go**." We read the "**g**" according to what follows it. Except for approximately 20 words that are exceptions, we usually read the **ge**, **gi**, and **gy** soft.

Soft ge, gi, gy

Read the **ge**, **gi** and **gy** soft like **j** or like the name of the letter **G**:

ge says j

lar**ge**	ca**ge**	sta**ge**
dan·**ge**r	mes·sa**ge**	mes·sen·**ge**r
le**g**·ends	col·le**ge**	ca*b*·ba**ge**
mar·ria**ge**	ju*d***ge**	fu*d***ge**
bri*d***ge**	**ge**rm	**ge**rms
Ger·man	**Ge**or**ge**	**ge**n·ius
gel·a·tin	**ge**n·der	**ge**n·er·al
an·**ge**l	le*d***ge**·er	mer**g**·er

38

gi says ji

gin	en·gine	en·gi·neer
or·i·gin	or·i·gin·al	gin·ger
gist	mag·ic	rig·id
gi·ant	gi·raffe	

gy says jy

stin·gy	prod·i·gy	gym
gym·nast	gyp·sy	E·gypt
as·trol·o·gy	psy·chol·o·gy	bi·ol·o·gy

This is the end of soft G!

Hard G The "**g**" is **hard** and it does not sound like the name of the letter **G** when followed by **a**, **o**, **u**, a consonant, or when not followed by anything as in "ba**g**." Read the ga, go, gu, gl, gr, g*h*, gg, and the final g like hard "g" in these words:

Hard G
ga, go, gu, gl,
gr, gh, gg, final g

ga

gas	gar·lic	gar·den
ga·rage	beg·gar	game
gal·ax·y	or·gan	or·gan·ic
en·gaged	kin·der·gar·ten	gal·ler·y

go

go	a·go	car·go
Chi·ca·go	got	God
gold	gov·ern	ghost

gu

gum	gun	guts
guy	guess	guest
gui·tar	guilt·y	guild
guar·an·tee	plague	gulf

gl

glad   glass   glue
gleam   glance   globe

gr

grass   grasp   grab
gross   gram·mar   a·gree
dis·a·gree   green   grin

gh

spa·ghet·ti   ghost   ghet·to

gg

eggs   logged   hugged

final g

bag   beg   leg
big   jog   jug
hug   fig   gang
wig   big·wig   twig

gn says n Read the "**g**" flowed by an "**n**" as a silent "**g**":

si**gn**	as·si**gn**	de·si**gn**
re·si**gn**	for·**ei**gn	

Hard ge, gi, gy

Read aloud many times until you memorize these **exceptions** of the hard **ge**, **gi**, and **gy**:

g**e**t	tar·g**e**t	for·g**e**t
fin·**ger**	lon·**ger**	sin**g**·er
gear	**ge**es**e**	**gi**v**e**
girl	**gi**r·dle	**gi**ll
gift	**gi**rth	**gi**z·zard
gid·dy	**gi**m·mick	**gi**g
gig·gle	**gy**·ne·col·o·gy	

Good work! You read 139 "G" words.

✗ Continue to **avoid** teaching any words that contain **qu**, **s** like **z** (ha**s**), some two vowels in a word (**au**to), most long words, words with suffixes (**tion**), words with prefixes (**un**), and simply stick with the order of words listed in this book.

Lesson 5: The **S** that sounds like a **Z**

Usually, a single "s" sounds like a "z" at the **end** of some small one-syllable words like "ha**s**." One "**s**" is usually too weak to keep its sound, and this is the reason we see so many small words ending with "**ss**" instead of one "**s**" as in "cla**ss**."

S says Z Read the "**s**" like a "**z**" when at the end of some short words like these:

is	his	as
has	was	Ms.
dogs	pens	ribs
plays	boys	keys
girls	goes	toes
trans	trans·late	trans·mit

Rule: A single "**s**" usually sounds like a "**z**" when **between** two vowels as in "ri**s**e." One "**s**" between two vowels is usually too weak to keep its sound, and if we need to hear the sound of "s" between two vowels, we often use soft a "c" as in "ri**c**e" and as in "de**c**ision."

S says Z Read the "**s**" between two vowels like "**z**" in these words:

rose	hose	nose
pose	close	dose
wise	rise	used
use (v.)	a·buse (v.)	clos·et
a·muse	mu·se·um	mu·sic

pres·ent   des·ert   re·sult

de·sire   sur·prise   com·pro·mise

You read 39 "S" words!

⚠ Continue to avoid teaching any words that contain **qu**, some of the two vowels in a word (b**oo**k), most long words, words with suffixes (**tion**), words with prefixes (**un**), and simply stick with the order of lessons presented in this book.

Lesson 6: The Q sounds like K

Q **Rule:** Every "**q**" is followed by a "**u**." Every "**q**" sounds like a **K**, and the "**qu**" sounds like "**kw**." Because the "**u**" is not a vowel in "**qu**," you must always look for a vowel after every "**qu**" as in "**qu**iz."

qu says kw

Read aloud the "**qu**" like "**kw**" aloud and look for a vowel after the "**qu**":

qu + i

quick	**qu**ick·er	**qu**ick·est
quick·ly	**qu**ilt	**qu**it
quits	ac·**qu**it	ac·**qu**its
quiz	**qu**izzed	e·**qu**ipped
e·**qu**ip·ment	e·**qu**iv·a·len·cy	e**q**·**u**i·ty
li**q**·**u**id	li**q**·**u**i·fy	in·**qu**ir·y
s**qu**ir·rel	**qu**ite	**qu**i·et
quire	ac·**qu**ire	re·**qu**ire
re·**qu**ires	re·**qu**ired	re·**qu**ir·ing

qu + e

quest	re·quest	con·quest
fre·quent	fre·quent·ly	fre·quen·cy
in·fre·quent	ban·quet	se·quence
se·quenced	que·ry	squeal
queen	con·se·quent·ly	el·o·quent

qu + a

qual·i·ty	e·qual·i·ty	qual·i·fy
squash	square	quart
quar·ter	quar·rel	quan·ti·ty
quail	ac·quaint·ances	e·qua·tor

qu + o

quote	quotes	quot·ed
quot·ing	quo·ta	quon·dam

ue The final "ue" after "q" is silent and it occurs at the end of a small number of words:

u·nique	tech·nique	an·tique
cri·tique	mys·tique	phy·sique
plaque		

u As in "mosq***u***ito," the "***u***" is silent in a small number of words:

con·q***u***er   con·q***u***er·or   col·lo·q***ui***·al

q***uo***·rum   mos·q***ui***·toes   liq·***u***or

Lesson 7: The **X** sounds like **Ks** or **Kc**

Rule: Anytime you hear yourself saying an "**s**" sound after the "**k**" sound, spell it with an "**x**," not with a "ks."

X = ks or kc

ax says aks

a***x***   fa***x***   fa***x***ed

wa***x***   wa***x***ed   ta***x***

ta***x***ed   ta***x***·ing   la***x***

re·la***x***   re·la***x***ed   Ma***x***

fla***x***   ma***x***·i·mum   sa***x***·o·phon*e*

ex says eks

e***x***-wif*e*   e***x***·cus*e*   e***x***·cus*e*d

e***x***·cus·ing   e***x***·e·cut*e*   e***x***·clud*e*

e***x***·clud·ing   e***x***·pos*e*   e***x***·pos·ing

e***x***·port   e***x***·plod*e*   e***x***·plod·ing

ex·pert ex·pire ex·pir·ing
ex·tinct ex·ter·mi·na·tor ex·ter·nal
ex·te·ri·or ex·crete ex·treme
ex·treme·ly ex·trem·ist ex·cel
ex·celled ex·cel·lent ex·cite
ex·cit·ed ex·cit·ing ex·cept
flex in·dex dup·lex
com·plex cor·tex text
text·book con·text ex·er·cise
an·o·rex·i·a dys·lex·i·a ex·it
ex·ile ex·am ex·act
ex·act·ly ex·empt ex·ag·ger·ate
ex·hi·bit ex·hi·bit·ing ex·hort

ix says iks

six six·ty sixty-six
six·teen mix mixed

mix·ing   mix·er   fix

fixed   fix·ing   fix·er

pre·fix   suf·fix   af·fix

ox says oks

box   boxed   box·ing

box·er   ox   ox·en

ox·y·gen   fox   fox·y

di·ox·ide   ap·prox·i·mate·ly

ux says uks

flux   in·flux   de·luxe

tux   tux·e·do   bux·om

You read 98 "q" and "x" words.

Read Instantly by Camilia Sadik

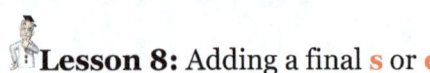

Lesson 8: Adding a final **s** or **es**

Adding s

Add an "**s**" to make plurals (pen**s**) or to add to verbs (play**s**):

-s

cat**s**	dog**s**	bed**s**
pen**s**	pin**s**	boy**s**
girl**s**	kid**s**	bag**s**
boat**s**	car**s**	hill**s**
stor**es**	hom**es**	snak**es**
run**s**	play**s**	add**s**
sniff**s**	sing**s**	win**s**
tub**s**	tell**s**	sell**s**
spell**s**	spill**s**	driv**es**
feel**s**	keep**s**	send**s**
hop**es**	b**uy**s	

Adding es

Add "**es**" instead of an "**s**" after **ss**, **ch**, **sh**, **x**, **zz**, and after some vowels:

-es

glass·**es**	class·**es**	lunch·**es**
teach·**es**	ash·**es**	wash·**es**
box·**es**	fix·**es**	fax·**es**
tax·**es**	mix·**es**	ex·cus·**es**
in·dex·**es**	quiz·z**es**	go**es**
po·ta·to**es**	mos·q*u*i·to**es**	

 Continue to avoid teaching any words that contain certain two vowels (h**au**l), any long words, words with suffixes (**tion**), words with prefixes (**un**), and simply stick with the order of words listed in this book.

Read Instantly by Camilia Sadik

Lesson 9: The final -**ve** and the prefix **ac**-

-ve Read aloud slowly to learn that a final "**v**" must be followed by a silent "**e**":

love	glove	a·bove
dove (n.)	dove (v.)	drove
grove	have	give
gives	live (v.)	lives
lived	love	loves
dive	save	saves
saved	shave	shaves
shaved	leave	leaves
ol·ive	ac·tive	cre·a·tive
sup·por·tive	de·serve	de·serves
de·served	ex·clu·sive	

ac- Read aloud to memorize the spelling of the prefix "**ac**" as in these words:

ac·cept	ac·ci·dent	ac·cess
ac·cent	ac·count	ac·cuse
ac·tive	ac·quit·ted	ac·quaint

Chapter 3: y, h, c, g, q, x, s, ve, ac

Reading Aloud is Imperative

Reading all the practice lessons aloud is imperative. Insist on students reading aloud. Explain to students, from the first day of class, that we acquire information through our five senses and show them how that works. Continue to insist until they read all the practice lessons aloud, whether in or outside of the classroom. If in a classroom, they need to read aloud together in one rhythm.

Students need to be convinced that when reading aloud, they are seeing the word, hearing it, and touching it in their mouths as they utter it. Not only does using the three senses together make learning possible, but it also speeds up the process. It is through the senses that any piece of information is registered into the memory portion of the brain.

Convince them to read aloud by narrating an example about an imaginary 10-year old child who was born with a perfect brain but without any of his five senses. Suppose that someone in the same room with that child poured hot coffee in a cup. How will the child learn what coffee is if he cannot see it or hear it pour or feel its heat or taste it or smell it? Naturally, the child would not learn what coffee means. By giving this example from the first day of class, you will convince your students that we acquire information through our senses.

The next step is to apply the child's example to learning to read and spell by using three of one's senses simultaneously. Students need to know that when reading aloud, they are seeing the word, hearing it, and feeling it in their mouths as they utter it. It is through the senses that any piece of information is registered into the memory portion of the brain. Without reading the practice lessons aloud, students will understand a spelling rule but will not remember the spelling of the words that follow that rule. Reading aloud is imperative for this method to work.

Teaching Instructions

✓ **You may now teach:**

✓ The hard **c**

✓ The hard **g**

✓ The **qu**

✓ The "**s**" that sounds like a "**z**"

✓ Any double consonants

✓ The "**y**" as a vowel

✓ Consonant blends

✓ The digraphs of "**h**"

✗ For the next chapter, please continue to **avoid** teaching the spelling patterns of phonics that have not yet been presented. You may check the following listing for which spelling pattern has not been introduced:

✗ **Avoid teaching:**

✗ Other two vowels in a word as in "**ou**t"

✗ Any long multi-syllabic words

✗ Any words with suffixes as in "na**tion**"

Simply stick with the order of lessons introduced then presented in this book. A number of other spelling patterns of phonics are still placed in a **queue** awaiting their turn to be introduced and presented in a number of words.

✗ Please **avoid** pressuring learners to write. They may begin to write letters and words after they finish reading this entire book aloud one time or as many times as needed until they achieve fluency in reading it. This book is mainly for learning to read phonics.

4 Affixes: tech-, -some, -cle, -cal, -tion, -sion, cian, and ătt

Lesson 1: -tech-, -some, -cle, -cal

tech- Read aloud slowly to memorize the spelling of the prefix "**tech–**" as in these words:

tech·nol·o·gy   tech·nol·o·gi·cal   tech·ni·cal

tech·ni·cal·ly   tech·nique   tech·niques

-some Read aloud slowly to memorize the spelling of the suffix –**some** as in these words:

han*d*·som*e*   lon*e*·som*e*   whol*e*·som*e*

tir*e*·som*e*   burden·som*e*   gru*e*·som*e*

-cle The suffixes –**cle** and –**cal**: As in "cy**cle**," the (consonant + le) ending usually makes **nouns**, and the "**le**" sounds like "**il**." For instance, "un**cle**" sounds like (unk~~il~~):

un·cle	cir·cle	ar·ti·cle
cy·cle	i·ci·cle	mir·a·cle
a·ble	ta·ble	cra·dle
a*p*·ple	sim·ple	li*t*·tle
ra*f*·fle	puz·zle	sin·gle
jun·gle	jun·gles	an·kle

-cal The "**-cal**" ending occurs in **adjectives**:

mag·i·**cal**	log·i·**cal**	prac·ti·**cal**
tech·ni·**cal**	his·tor·i·**cal**	po·lit·i·**cal**
po·lit·i·**ca*l*** ·ly	me·chan·i·**cal**	vo·**cal**

No Force Memorization is Needed

Learning to read and spell is acquired naturally, as students keep reading aloud slowly. They need to read aloud to see and hear the words; and they need to read slowly to see the way words are spelled and to avoid speed-reading. Forced speed-reading before learning to read and spell causes seeing and then spelling letters in reverse.

This book is designed to help beginners read and to give them an idea of how English letters are used to represent various sounds. More spelling rules with intense practice lessons are in the next book entitled, *Learn to Spell 500 Words a Day* by Camilia Sadik.

Lesson 2: The suffixes -**tion**, -**sion**, and -**cian**

The endings -**tion**, -**sion**, and **cian** sound the same. The -**tion** is used in most such words, the -**sion** is used in a small number of words (approximately 47 words), and the -**cian** is used in words that mean careers or hobbies (approximately 17 words).

-tion Use the -**tion** in the **vast majority** of words, as in:

na·**tion**	sta·**tion**	ac·**tion**
ed·u·ca·**tion**	ap·pli·ca·**tion**	va·ca·**tion**
im·mi·gra·**tion**	dis·tor·**tion**	lo·**tion**
no·**tion**	po·**tion**	

-sion Use the -**sion** in approximately **47** words mainly after "**ss**" as in "expre**ss**→expre**ss**ion" and in the word "mission" or in a word that contains "mission" as in:

mi*s*·**sion**	ad·mi*s*·**sion**	per·mi*s*·**sion**
e·mi*s*·**sion**	ex·pre*s*·**sion**	dis·cu*s*·**sion**
im·pre*s*·**sion**	ex·ten·**sion**	man·**sion**

-cian Use the -**cian** in approximately **17** words that mean careers or hobbies, as in:

| mu·si·**cian** | ma·gi·**cian** | phy·si·**cian** |
| pol·it·i·**cian** | e·lec·tri·**cian** | op·ti·**cian** |

Lesson 3: Doubling the consonants after short vowels (ătt, ĕpp, ĭnn, ŏbb, ŭgg)

 As in "di**nn**er," only two consonants (**nn**) can build a fence strong enough to keep "**i**" and "**e**" from helping each other. If we did not double the "**n**," a word like "di**nn**er" would become "di**n**er." Similarly, we need to double the "**t**" after the short "a" sound as in "fat→fa**tt**er→fa**tt**est." Read these words aloud slowly to help you remember to double the consonants after the short vowels:

after short ă

fat→fa*t*·ter→fa*t*·test

chat→cha*t*·ted→cha*t*·ting

nap→na**pp**ed→na*p*·ping

clap→cla**pp**ed→cla*p*·ping

wrap→wra**pp**ed→wra*p*·ping

glad→gla*d*·der→gla*d*·dest

mad→ma*d*·der→ma*d*·dest

sad→sa*d*·der→sa*d*·dest

ba*g*·gy→ba*g*·gi·er→ba*g*·gi·est

man→ma**nn**ed

ba**nn**ed→ba*n*·ning→ba*n*·ner

Dan→Da*n*·ny

after short ĕ

step→stepped→step·ping

get→get·ting→get·ter

pet→pet·ted→pet·ting

bet→bet·ted→bet·ting

wet→wet·ted→wet·ting

red→red·der→red·dest

Ben→Ben·ny

Fred→Fred·dy

begged→beg·ging→beg·gar

Ted→Ted·dy

mess·y→mess·i·er→mess·i·est

Ed→Ed·dy

spell→spelled→spell·ing

end→end·ed

after short ĭ

clip → clipped → clip·per

split → split·ting

din → din·ner

thin → thin·ner

be·gin → be·gin·ning

ac·quit → ac·quit·ted

after short ŏ

hot → hot·ter → hot·test

got → got·ten → for·got·ten

mop → mopped → mop·ping

stop → stopped → stop·ping

shop → shopped → shop·ping

hop → hopped → hop·ping

jog → jogged → jog·ging

rob → robbed → rob·ber·y

after short ŭ

cut→cut·ting→cut·ter

shut→shut·ting→shut·ter

hum→hummed→hum·ming

hug→hugged→hug·ging

scrub→scrubbed→scrub·bing

stuff→stuffed→stuff·ing

Yes! You can read!

Teaching Instructions

✅ **You may now teach:**

☑ The hard "**c**"
☑ The hard "**g**"
☑ The "**qu**"
☑ The "**s**" that sounds like "**z**"
☑ Double consonants
☑ The "**y**" as a vowel
☑ Consonant blends
☑ Digraphs of "**h**"
☑ The prefix "**tech-**"
☑ The endings "**-cle**" and "**-cal**"
☑ The suffix "**-tion**"
☑ The suffix "**-some**"
☑ Double consonants after short vowels

❌ For the next chapter, please continue to **avoid** teaching any spelling patterns that have not been introduced. Check the following listing for which spelling patterns of phonic have not yet been introduced:

❌ **Avoid teaching:**

❌ Other two vowel combinations in a word as in "br**ea**d"
❌ Any long multi-syllabic words
❌ Any words with suffixes not yet presented, like the "ture" in "cul**ture**"

Simply adhere to the order of lessons introduced and presented in this book.

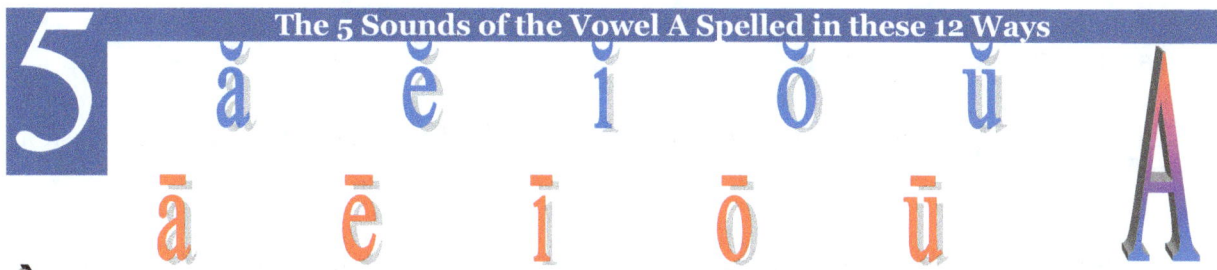

Lesson 1: The **five** sounds of "a" are spelled in **12** ways we call spelling patterns, as in r**a**n, r**ai**n, f**a**te, d**a**y, **a**ble, **ei**ght, **a**ll, **a**lways, **au**to, str**a**w, w**a**r, li**a**r.

✓ The vowel "a" has a unique short sound as in "m**a**n," a long sound as in "m**ai**n," a special sound as in "l**au**ndry," and a weak sound as in "li**a**r." Not only the "a" but each vowel has a unique **short** sound, a **long** sound, a **weak** sound, and a few **other** special sounds. The long sound of a vowel sounds like the letter name of that vowel.

The short **ă** as in r**a**n, f**a**t, and f**a**tter is a unique sound that does not sound like the name of the letter **A**—it is followed by one or two consonant as in "f**a**t" and "f**a**tter."

The long **ā** sounds like the name of the letter **A** (ay), and it is spelled in five ways we call spelling patterns, , as in r**ai**n, f**a**te, d**a**y, t**a**ble, and **ei**ght.

The short **ĕ** as in b**e**t, b**e**tted, and b**e**tting is a unique sound that does not sound like the name of the letter **E**—it is followed by one or two consonant as in "b**e**t" and "b**e**tting."

The long **ē** sounds like the name of the letter **E**, and it is spelled in 10 ways we call spelling patterns, as in m**ee**t, m**ea**t, P**e**te, ch**ie**f, rec**ei**ve, monk**ey**, luck**y**, m**e**, pet**i**te, and sk**i**.

The short **ĭ** as in s**i**t, s**i**tter, and s**i**tting is a unique sound that does not sound like the name of the letter **I**—it is followed by one or two consonant as in "s**i**t" and "s**i**tter."

The long **ī** sounds like the name of the letter **I**, and it is spelled in 10 major ways we call spelling patterns, as in h**i**, h**igh**, s**ign**, f**i**nd, sk**y**, d**ie**, d**ye**, b**i**te, t**y**pe, and c**y**·cle.

The short **ŏ** as in h**o**t, h**o**tter, and h**o**ttest is a unique sound that does not sound like the name of the letter **O**—it is followed by one or two consonant as in "h**o**t" and "h**o**tter."

The long **ō** sounds like the name of the letter **O**, and it is spelled in these seven major ways we call spelling patterns: sn**ow**, t**oe**, s**ou**l, b**oa**t, h**o**pe, n**o**, and c**o**ld.

The short **ŭ** as in c**u**t, c**u**tter, and c**u**tting is a unique sound that does not sound like the name of the letter **U**—it is followed by one or two consonant as in "c**u**t" and "c**u**tter."

The long **ū** sounds like the name of the letter **U**, but it can sound like y**oo** as in "men**u**" or like **oo** as in "bl**ue**"—it is spelled in seven major spelling patterns, as in bl**ue**, s**ui**t, f**eu**d, f**ew**, c**u**te, men·**u**, and z**oo**.

Read Instantly by Camilia Sadik

Lesson 2: The short ă as in "man"

ă The short ă is this unique sound that does not sound like the name of the letter **A**. The short ă is followed by one or two consonant as in "f**a**t" and "f**a**tt**er**."

Read aloud and focus on the one consonant or two that follow the short vowel ă:

ran	man	man·ner	Dan	fan	tan
Jan	ban	pan	van	hat	sat
bat	mat	pat	rat	fat	fat·ter
bad	fad	sad	had	mad	pad
dad	bag	rag	nag	Sam	Pam
dam	ram	nap	napped	lap	map
tap	zap	Al	Hal	pal	pals
ad	add	ad·ded	fax	wax	tax

Chapter 5: Phonics Made by A

Lesson 3: The long ā sound is spelled in these five ways: ray, rain, ate, a´·ble, eight

1. The long ā sound as in "day"

ay says ā The long ā sound is spelled with the "ay" phonic at the end of words.

Read aloud slowly all the practice lessons in this book and focus your vision on the vowels:

day	bay	hay	Jay	ray	tray
may	way	play	played	play·ing	lay
slay	clay	stay	stayed	stay·ing	pray
prayed	pray·ing	gray	o·kay	pay	say

sunrays

sway

bay

play

Ray   Jay

65

Read Instantly by Camilia Sadik

2. The long ā sound as in "rain"

ai says ā The long ā sound spelled with the "ai" phonic inside words: When two vowels are walking, the first one does the talking. This means that as in "rain," when the two vowels "a" and "i" are next to each other (walking) in a stressed syllable, the first one "a" does the talking by saying its letter name **A** and the second one "**i**" is silent.

main	rain	brain	train	drain	grain
strain	pain	Spain	lain	slain	plain
ex·plain	gain	vain	mail	nail	snail
pail	jail	hail	sail	fail	bail
wail	tail	trail·er	faith	chain	stain
main·tain	ob·tain	paint	faint	saint	aid
aide	maid	raid	braid	af·raid	aim
claim	wait	bait	straight	raise	raised

Compare the short ă with long ā in these words:

man, main	pan, pain	ran, rain	bran, brain
van, vain	plan, plain	mad, maid	Brad, braid
pad, paid	am, aim	bat, bait	pal, pail

66

3. The long ā sound as in "cake"

a-e says ā The long ā sound spelled with "a-e" as in "fate": As in "fate," the two vowels (a-e) can still help one another when there is only one consonant "t" between them. The one "t" is too weak to keep the two vowels from helping each other (walking together). The first vowel "a" does the talking, while the second vowel "e" is silent. This explains the reason for doubling the consonants, as in fat→fatter→fattest; one consonant "t" between two vowels is too **weak** and we need two consonants "tt" to keep the two vowels from walking together.

hate	fate	rate	mate	late	plate
Kate	state	date	ate	made	fade
bake	cake	take	snake	grade	trade
tape	grape	shape	ale	sale	tale
stale	male	fe·male	whale	in·hale	ex·hale
name	fame	same	shame	came	be·came
game	blame	Jane	sane	in·sane	cane
lane	air·plane	Dave	gave	save	shave
brave	grave	ace	face	race	trace
gaze	phase	phrase	gage	en·gage	vase
base	case	e·rase			

Compare short ă with long ā in these words:

fat, fate	hat, hate	rat, rate	mat, mate
at, ate	cat, Kate	fad, fade	mad, made
Sam, same	pal, pale	mal, male	plan, plane
Jan, Jane	can, cane		
tap, tape	cap, cape		
back, bake	shack, shake		
snack, snake	Jack, Jake		
Mack, make	lack, lake		

Jake, lake, cake, bake, milkshake

4. The long ā sound as in "able"

a´·says ā The long ā sound spelled with a stressed final "a" as in "a´·ble."

Read aloud slowly and focus on the stressed long "a" at the end of syllables:

a´·ble	ta´·ble	ca´·ble	fa´·tal
na´·sal	A´·pril	a´·pron	a´·li·en
cra´·dle	ma´·ple	pa´·per	ba´·by
Ma´·bel	na´·tion	do·na´·tion	

5. The long ā sound as in "eight"

ei says ā The long ā sound spelled with the "ei" phonic as in "eight": A minor way to spell the long ā sound is with "ei" as in "eight" and that is to tell two words like "ate" and "eight" apart. Once the "ei" phonic was used to tell two words apart, more words ended up being spelled with it:

eight	weight	weigh	their
vein	reign	rein	neigh·bor
beige	Bei·rut	sur·veil·lance	veil

Compare:
| eight, ate | weight, wait | weigh, way | their, there |
| vein, vain | reign, rein, rain | | |

Read Instantly by Camilia Sadik

Lesson 4: The special sounds of "a" spelled in these **five** ways: **all**, s**a**lt, s**aw**, **au**to, w**a**r
The vowel "**a**" has a special sound that is spelled in these four ways we call spelling patterns: **all**, **al**so, s**aw**, **au**to. Usually, the "a+ll" occurs at the end of short one-syllable words as in "t**all**" and the "a+l" occurs at the beginning or in the middle of words as in "**al**ways." The "**aw**" sounds like one unit (one sound) and so does the "**au**." Usually, the "**au**" does not occur at the end of words, but the "**aw**" does.

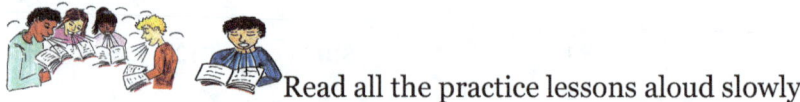 Read all the practice lessons aloud slowly.

1. The special sound of "**a**" as in "**all**"

a+ll The special sound of "**a**" spelled with the "**a+ll**" phonic: Technically, the "a+ll" is spelled like the short "a" but it does not sound like short "a" because the "l" controls the sound of "a" and changes it to this special sound, as in these words:

all	w**all**	b**all**	b**all**s
f**all**	f**all**s	h**all**	c**all**
m**all**	m**all**s	st**all**	in·st**all**

F**all**

Niagara F**all**s

footb**all** team

2. The special sound of "a" as in "always"

a+l The special sound of "a" spelled with the "a+l" phonic: Technically, the "a+l" is spelled like the short "a" but it does not sound like short "a" because the "l" controls the sound of "a" and changes it to this special sound, as in these words:

al·ways	**al**·so	**al**·most	**al**·ter
al·tar	W**al**·ter	W**al**tz	w**al**·nut
s**al**t	h**al**t	b**al**d	f**al**se
w**al**k	t**al**k	with·draw·**al**	

3. The special sound of "a" as in "draw"

aw The same special sound of "a" spelled with the "**aw**" phonic: The "aw" sounds like one unit, unlike the "a" and unlike the "w." Don't say the "a" and don't say the "w" because both letters blend together to make a single special sound that is sometimes confused with the sound of an "o," as in these words:

l**aw**	dr**aw**	str**aw**	r**aw**
s**aw**	j**aw**	th**aw**	p**aw**s
y**aw**n	d**aw**n	p**aw**n	l**aw**n
h**aw**k	sh**aw**l	col*e*·sl**aw**	**aw**k·ward
awn·ing	**aw**·ful		

Strawberries

Dawn

coleslaw

prawn

raw veggies

4. The special sound of "a" as in "auto"

au The same special sound of "a" spelled with the "au" phonic: The "au" sounds like one unit, unlike the "a" and unlike the "u." Don't say the "a" and don't say the "u" because both letters blend together to make a single special sound that is sometimes confused with the sound of an "o," as in these words:

Paul	haul	fault	vault
cause	be·cause	taught	caught
daugh·ter	au·to	Au·gust	auc·tion
au·thor	as·sault	sauce	fau·cet
res·tau·rant	Tau·rus	laun·dry	gauze
launch	launched	haunt	haunt·ed

5. A minor special sound of "a" as in "warm"

w+a+r The special sound of "a" as in "war": The "a" between "w" and "r" has this special sound that is sometimes confused with the sound of an "o," as in these words:

war	warm	warn	wart
a·ward	re·ward	re·ward·ed	war·den
for·ward	back·ward	quar·ter	quar·rel

About this Learning Method: Don't worry about learning to spell every single word that you read. Don't stop too long for every small detail. Simply, keep reading aloud and learning will take place naturally, without forced memorization. Learning occurs without you having to pay too much attention to it. In time, and as you use these words, their spelling will sink in.

Chapter 5: Phonics Made by A

Lesson 5: The weak sound of "a" as in "liar"

As in "beggar," the sound of "a" is weak because it falls in a syllable that is not stressed. This weak sound of a vowel is called a "schwa" sound, and its dictionary symbol is like an upside-down **e** like this ə.

Read aloud these words that contain the schwa sound of "a" and notice that the stress can be on any of the other syllables, but not on the syllable where the "a" is:

beg´·gar	bur´·glar	sin·gu·lar	sim·i·lar
pop·u·lar	li·ar	al·tar	vul·gar
sum·ma·ry	sec·re·tar·y	sep·a·rate	drun·kard

75

Teaching Instructions

✓ **You may now teach:**

✓ The hard "**c**"
✓ The hard "**g**"
✓ The "**qu**"
✓ The "**s**" that sounds like "**z**"
✓ Double consonants
✓ The "**y**" as a vowel
✓ Consonant blends
✓ The digraphs of "**h**"
✓ The prefix "**tech-**"
✓ The endings "**-cle**" and "**-cal**"
✓ The suffix "**-tion**"
✓ The suffix "**-some**"
✓ Double consonants after short vowels
✓ Words that contain the long **ā** sound as in: r**ay**, r**ai**n, **ate**, **a**ble, **ei**ght
✓ The special sounds of "**a**" as in t**all**, s**al**t, s**aw**, **au**to, and w**ar**

✗ For the next chapter, please continue to **avoid** teaching some of the spelling patterns of phonics that have not yet been introduced. Check the following listing for which spelling pattern has not yet been introduced:

✗ **Avoid teaching:**

✗ Vowel combinations that have not been introduced, as in "thr**ea**d"
✗ Any long multi-syllabic words
✗ Any words with suffixes not yet presented, like the "ture" in "cul**ture**."

Simply adhere to the order of lessons introduced and presented in this book. For now, the rest of the spelling patterns of phonics are placed in a **queue** awaiting their turn to be introduced one-at-a-time. The order of the lessons is carefully planned, and no words are thrown randomly at people to learn.

Chapter 6: Phonics Made by E

The 4 Sounds of the Vowel E are Spelled in these 17 Ways

Lesson 1: The **four** sounds of "e" are spelled in **17** ways we call spelling patterns

✓ The vowel **E** has a short sound as in "m**e**t," a long sound as in "m**ea**t," other minor sounds as "**e**nough," and a weak sound as in "carpent**e**r."

The short **ĕ** is a unique sound that does not sound like the name of the letter **E**, and it is followed by one or two consonant as in "l**e**t" and "l**e**tter."

The short **ĕ** is also spelled with an "**ea**" as in "br**ea**d." The people who developed written English may have used this "**ea**" pattern to tell apart two words like "br**e**d" and "br**ea**d," and once this "**ea**" pattern was used, more words were spelled with it.

The long **ē** sounds like name of the letter **E**, and it is spelled in **10** spelling patterns, as in m**ee**t, m**ea**t, P**e**t**e**, bel**ie**ve, rec**ei**ve, monk**ey**, luck**y**, m**e**, sk**i**, and el**i**t**e**.

77

Lesson 2: The short ĕ spelled in two ways: "brĕd" and "brĕad"

1. The short ĕ sound as in "brĕd"

 The short ĕ is followed by one or two consonant as in "wĕt" and "wĕtter." The short ĕ is a unique sound that does not sound like the name of the letter **E**.

 Read aloud and concentrate on the one or two consonants that follow the short ĕ:

met	set	bet	pet	wet	vet
yet	let	jet	get	ten	men
pen	hen	Ben	Ken	yes	less
mess	dress	chess	guess	guest	Ed
Ted	bed	red	fed	med	led
bled	fled	wed	web	step	swept
chef	tell	fell	bell	well	cell
sell	spell	spell·ing			

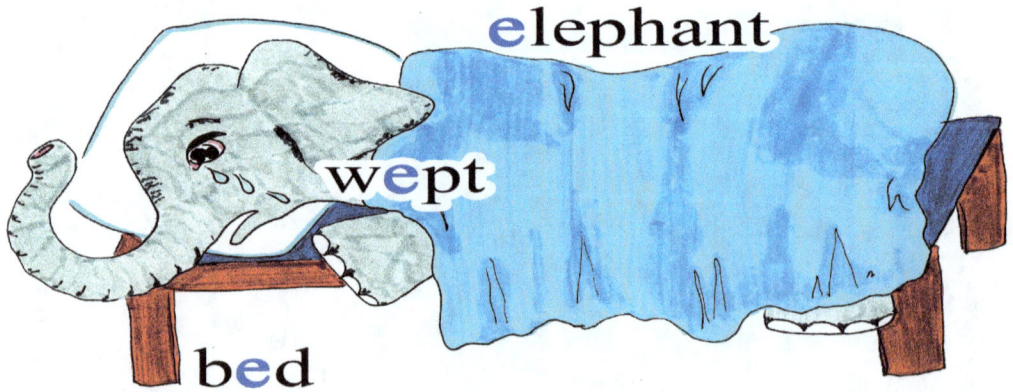

Eddie's story — elephant, wept, bed

78

2. The short ĕ sound as in "brĕad"

 The people who developed written English may have used this "ea" pattern to tell apart two words like "bred" and "bread." However and once this "ea" pattern was used, more words were spelled with it.

 Read aloud slowly:

head	dead	read	bread	thread	spread
dread	al·read·y	stead·y	in·stead	lead	death
breath	leath·er	feath·er	weath·er	Heath·er	sweat
sweat·er	threat	health	wealth	dealt	heav·y
deaf	meas·ure	pleas·ure	pleas·ant	earth	ear·ly
learn	heard	search	searched	search·es	meant

Compare and read aloud:

red, read   led, lead   herd, heard   bred, bread

wheth·er, weath·er

sweating

sweater

Heather

leather

thread

treadmill

Read Instantly by Camilia Sadik

**Lesson 3:** The long ē spelled in **10** ways

 The long ē sounds like name of the letter **E**, and it is spelled in these **10** spelling patterns we call phonics: m**ee**t, m**ea**t, P**e**t**e**, bel**ie**ve, rec**ei**ve, monk**ey**, luck**y**, m**e**, sk**i**, and el**i**t**e**.

1. The long ē sound as in "m**ee**t"

 As in "m**ee**t," when the two vowels "**ee**" are walking, the first "**e**" does the talking and the second "**e**" is silent. The silent "**e**" is there just to help the first "**e**" sound long.

 Read all the practice lessons aloud slowly. Concentrate on the long ē spelled with "**ee**":

m**ee**t	f**ee**t	b**ee**t	sh**ee**t	str**ee**t	sw**ee**t
gr**ee**t	D**ee**	s**ee**	b**ee**	f**ee**	fr**ee**
tr**ee**	thr**ee**	n**ee**d	f**ee**d	bl**ee**d	s**ee**d
br**ee**d	gr**ee**d	cr**ee**d	sp**ee**d	st**ee**d	suc·c**ee**d
t**ee**th	t**ee**th*e*	d**ee**p	k**ee**p	j**ee**p	b**ee**p
s**ee**p	sh**ee**p	sl**ee**p	sw**ee**p	w**ee**k	s**ee**k
p**ee**k	t**ee**n	t**ee**n·ager	scr**ee**n	s**ee**n	self-est**ee**m

Compare and read aloud:
m**e**t, m**ee**t   f**e**d, f**ee**d   sl**e**pt, sl**ee**p   sw**e**pt, sw**ee**p

2. The long ē sound as in "m**ea**t"

ea says ē As in "m**ea**t," when the two vowels "**ea**" are walking, the first one "**e**" does the talking and the second one "**a**" is silent. The silent "**a**" is there just to help the first "**e**" sound long.

 Read all the practice lessons aloud slowly. Concentrate on the long ē spelled with "**ea**":

m**ea**t	**ea**t	s**ea**t	b**ea**t	n**ea**t	h**ea**t
tr**ea**t	y**ea**st	wh**ea**t	s**ea**	t**ea**	p**ea**
p**ea**·nut	r**ea**d	l**ea**d	ch**ea**p	r**ea**p	w**ea**k
p**ea**k	b**ea**k	bl**ea**k	fr**ea**k	sn**ea**k	sp**ea**k
l**ea**sh	t**ea**ch	**ea**ch	p**ea**ch	im·p**ea**ch	b**ea**ch
bl**ea**ch	r**ea**ch	h**ea**l	st**ea**l	v**ea**l	m**ea**l
t**ea**m	dr**ea**m	cr**ea**m	st**ea**m	f**ea**st	b**ea**st
b**ea**n	m**ea**n	cl**ea**n	d**ea**n	**ea**r	h**ea**r

 Compare and read aloud:

m**e**t, m**ea**t   s**e**t, s**ea**t   n**e**t, n**ea**t   m**e**n, m**ea**n

m**ea**t   b**ea**ns   wh**ea**t br**ea**d   p**ea** soup   st**ea**med s**ea**food   p**ea**ches   ice cr**ea**m

3. The long ē sound as in "Pete"

e-e says ē Compare "pet" with "Pete." The second "e" helps the first one to be long ē. The two vowels can still help each other when there is only one consonant between them. One consonant between two vowels is too weak to keep the two vowels from helping each other (walking together).

Read all the practice lessons aloud slowly. Concentrate on the long ē spelled with "e-e":

Pete	com·pete	com·plete	con·crete
ath·lete	Steve	Eve	Gene
here	mere	sin·cere	these
Jap·a·nese	Chi·nese	Le·ba·nese	Vi·et·nam·ese
theme	ex·treme	in·ter·vene	pre·cede
im·pede			

Compare and read aloud:
pet, Pete   them, theme

4. The long ē sound as in "elite"

i-e says ē As in "elite," the long ē occurs in this spelling pattern (*i* + consonants + *e*) in a small number of words:

Read all the practice lessons aloud slowly. Concentrate on the long ē spelled with "*i-e*":

e·lit*e*	pe·tit*e*	po·lic*e*	ma·chin*e*
rou·tin*e*	mag·a·zin*e*	gas·o·lin*e*	ma·rin*e*
lim·o*u*·sin*e*			

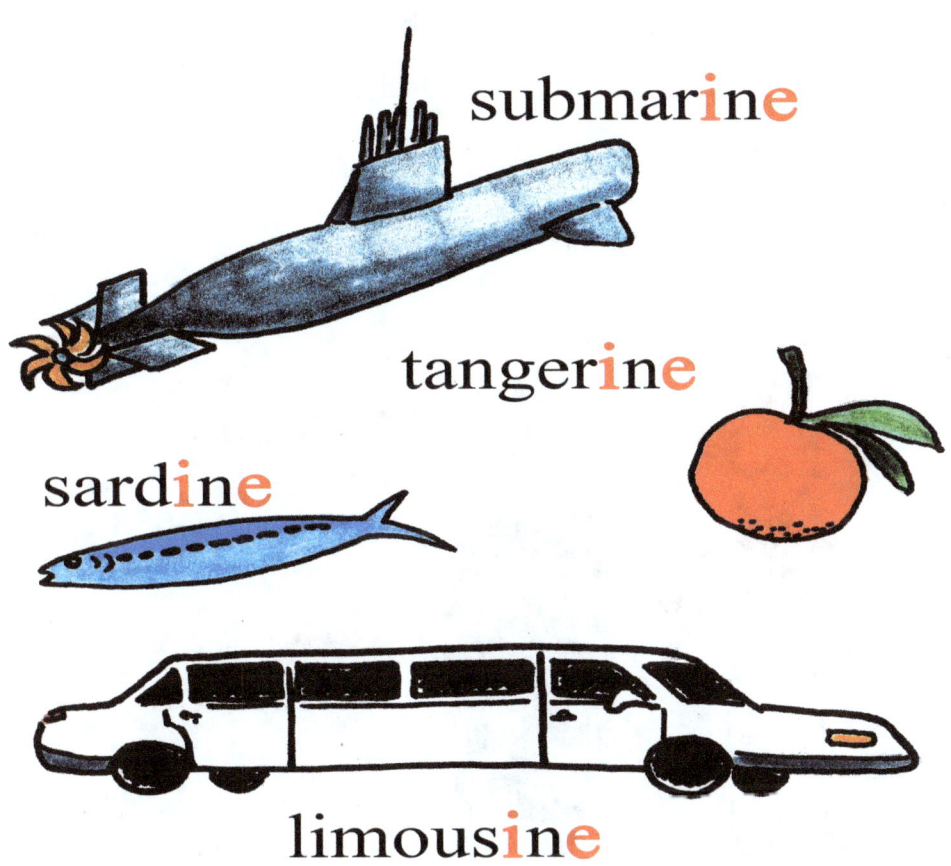

submarine

tangerine

sardine

limousine

5. The long ē sound as in "chief"

ie says ē As in "chief," the "ie" says long ē. Memorize this ☞ i before e except after c.

 Read aloud slowly and notice that the "ie" phonic is often followed by an "f" or a "v":

chief	thief	be·lief	re·lief
brief	grief	be·lieve	thieves
grieve	a·chieve	niece	piece
pierce	fierce	cash·ier	pier
priest	field	shield	yield
mov·ie	cal·o·rie	Jack·ie	ge·nie

 Compare and read aloud:
niece, nice   chef, chief

6. The long ē sound as in "receive"

ei says ē As in "receive," the "ei" after "c" sounds like long ē, and we use "ei" instead of "ie" after "c" in this small number of words.

Read aloud slowly and notice that the "ei" phonic being mainly after "c":

ceil·ing	re·ceive	re·ceipt	de·ceive
con·ceive	con·ceit	con·ceit·ed	de·ceit
pro·tein			

7. The long ē sound as in "key"

ey says ē As in "mon**ey**," the "-**ey**" is in approximately **30** words, and the 30 words are specific **nouns**. The "-**ey**" occurs after a "k" as in "mon**key**," after "l" as in "val**ley**," and after one "n" as in "mon**ey**."

 Read aloud slowly and notice that the "**ey**" phonic is only in nouns after **k, l** and one **n**:

mon·**key**	don·**key**	tur·**key**	**key**
mo**n**·**ey**	ho**n**·**ey**	kid·**ney**	at·tor·**ney**
chim·**ney**	val·**ley**	al·**ley**	vol·**ley**·ball
pars·**ley**	bar·**ley**	trol·**ley**	

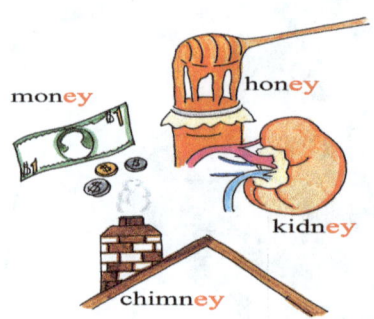

Chapter 6: Phonics Made by E

8. The long ē sound as in "city"

y says ē As in "city," the "y" at the end of long words sounds like long ē.

Read aloud slowly. If you read silently, you may understand but not memorize the spelling of the words you read.

cit·y	par·ty	emp·ty	bus·y
hap·py	Den·ny	slow·ly	sad·ly
mad·ly	luck·y	luck·i·ly	risk·y

9. The long ē sound as in "he"

e´ says ē As in "me´" and as in "me´·di·a," one "e" at the end of a short word or at the end of a stressed syllable, sounds like long ē. In a few words, one "e" at the end of a long word sounds like a long ē as in "apostrophe."

we	he	she	be
me	me·di·a	de·cent	vid·e·o
ste·re·o	i·de·a	se·ries	se·ri·ous
se·cret	re·cess	pre·fix	e·go
fre·quent	ve·to	fe·ver	e-mail
the·o·ry	the·a·ter	ar·e·a	mu·se·um
ac·ne	rec·i·pe	a·pos·tro·phe	

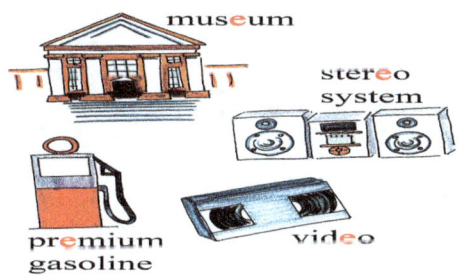

museum
stereo system
premium gasoline
video

10. The long ē sound as in "ski"

i says ē As in "ra·di·o," the long ē sound can occur in "i" at the end of **second** or **third** syllables.

 Read aloud slowly and notice that this "i" phonic is mainly in the second or third syllable:

sk**i**	me·d**i**·a	ra·d**i**·o	stu·d**i**·o
sta·d**i**·um	me·d**i**·um	spa·g*het*·t**i**	v**i**·sa
mac·a·ro·n**i**	a·l**i**·en	min·**i**·bus	ma·te·r**i**·al
se·r**i**·al	se·r**i**·ous	u·to·p**i**·a	

Chapter 6: Phonics Made by E

Lesson 4: The weak sound of "e" as in "cemet e ry"

As in "cemetery," the third "e" has a weak sound because it is in a syllable that is unstressed. This weak sound of a vowel is called a schwa sound; its dictionary symbol is ə.

Read aloud and notice that other syllables may be stressed in a word but not the syllable where the schwa is:

cem·e·ter·y	fas′·ten	driv·en	tur·ner
cu·cum·ber	hun·ter	po·em	po·et·ry
ev·i·dence	sou·ve·nir	in·no·cent	an·them
trail·er	car·pen·ter	sum·mer·y	en·er·gy
lit·er·al			

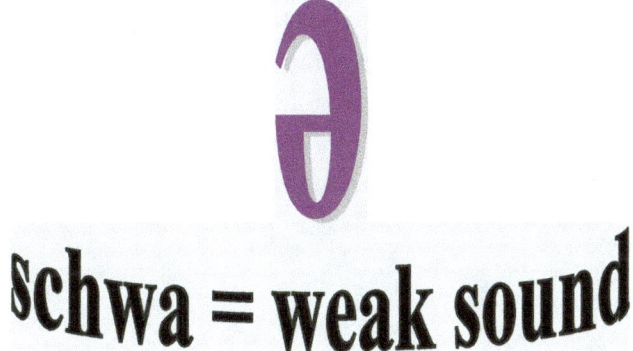

schwa = weak sound

x Continue to avoid teaching any words that contain certain two vowels (suit), which are not yet presented, most long words, words with suffixes not yet presented, words with prefixes not yet presented, and simply adhere to the order of words listed in this book.

Homework

Say two or more words for each sound and each spelling pattern that contains:

1. The short ĕ as in met, spell,

2. The short ĕ as in head, meant,

3. The long ē as in meet, see,

4. The long ē as in meat, team,

5. The long ē as in Pete, Japanese,

6. The long ē as in happy, lucky,

7. The long ē as in monkey, money, alley,

8. The long ē as in receipt,

9. The long ē as in chief, believe,

10. The long ē as in he, media,

Chapter 7: Phonics Made by I

The 8 Sounds of the Vowel I are Spelled in these 19 Ways

Lesson 1: The **eight** sounds of "**i**" are spelled in **19** ways we call spelling patterns

✓ The vowel **I** has a short sound as in "s**i**t," a long sound as in "s**i**t**e**," special sounds as in "so**ci**al," and a weak sound as in "test**i**fy."

The short **ĭ** is a unique sound that does not sound like the name of the letter **I**; it is followed by one or two consonant as in "t**i**p" and "t**i**ppe**d**."

y says ĭ The short **i** is also spelled with a "**y**" as in "g**y**m." This pattern may have been originally used to tell apart two words like "**J**im" and "g**y**m," and once this "**y**" spelling pattern was used, more words were spelled with it.

The long **ī** sounds like name of the letter **I**, and it is spelled in **10** ways we call spelling patterns, as in m**y**, h**igh**, s**ign**, fi**l**e, st**y**le, c**y**´·cle, m**i**ld, t**ie**, d**ye**, and h**i**.

Read Instantly by Camilia Sadik

Lesson 2: The short ĭ spelled in *two* ways: "Jim" and "gym"

1. The short ĭ sound as in "Jim"

The short ĭ is a unique sound that does not sound like the name of the letter **I**–it is followed by one or two consonant as in "sip" and "sipped." Read aloud and concentrate on the one or two consonants that follow the short ĭ:

sit	bit	kit	lit
hit	pit	fit	wit
it	did	bid	hid
lid	bib	lib	rib
hip	sip	sipped	lip
tip	him	dim	Tim
Jim	gym	rim	slim
slim·mer	lit·ter	bit·ter	bin
sin	din	din·ner	win
win·ner	kin	fin	tin
in	inn	in·ning	be·gin
be·gin·ning	six	mix	fix
clip	clipped	clip·per	

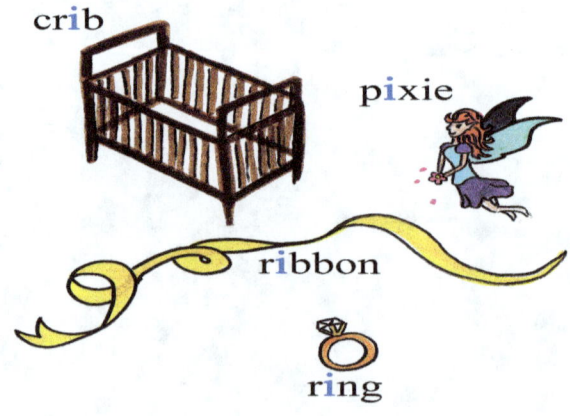

crib
pixie
ribbon
ring

2. The short ĭ sound as in "gym"

y says ĭ The short ĭ spelled with "y" as in "gym" may have been used to tell apart two words like "Jim" and "gym," and once the "y" pattern was used, more words were spelled with it.
Read aloud and concentrate on the short ĭ:

gym	cyst	sys·tem	sym·bol
symp·toms	mys·ter·y	Cyn·thi·a	Lynn
phys·ics	hys·ter·i·a	dys·lex·i·a	an·a·lyst
hyp·no·tize	gyp·sy	E·gypt	pyr·a·mid
typ·i·cal	syl·la·ble		

 Compare and read aloud:

Jim went to the gym.

Bill paid his bill.

The ba·by's bib is in her crib.

Which exit takes us to the witch's house?

Sib·yl has two syl·la·bles in her name.

Sib·yl has six sib·lings.

You don't make prof·it by be·ing a proph·et.

The kid needs help; he grew up on skid row.

Skid row is an id·i·om from Eng·lish slang.

Are you ly·ing to me or are you ly·ing down?

Lynn stayed in the same inn in which I was stay·ing.

There is a rip in my slip.

I dropped my pin in the bin.

I know the trick to help words stick.

The chick·en is in the kitch·en.

Is a pix·ie a fairy·like crea·ture?

Take off your ring and wring out the clothes.

To live I need to be a·ble to give.

Don't bid your mon·ey like I did!

Lesson 3: The long ī spelled in 10 ways

1. The long ī sound as in "my"

y says ī The long ī sounds like the name of the letter **I**. The first example is the "y" at the end of small, mainly one-syllable words. Read all the practice lessons aloud slowly. Concentrate on the long ī spelled with "y" at the end of short words:

my	sky	try	fry
cry	dry	pry	why
by	buy	guy	shy
sly	ply	re·ply	re·ly

skyscrapers

plywood

fry fish

2. The long ī sound as in "high"

igh says ī A silent "gh" after an "i" makes the "i" long. Read aloud and focus on the long ī spelled with "i+gh" in these words:

night	knight	sight	in·sight
light	slight	right	bright
might	tight	fight	flight
high	thigh	sigh	

nightlight

midnight

knight

bright highlighter

flight time
12:00am

3. The long ī sound as in "sign"

ign says īn A "silent g + n" after an "i" make the "i" long, mainly in words that contain the word "sign."

sign   signed   de·sign   as·sign

con·sign·ment   re·sign   be·nign   a·lign·ment

assignments

sign design

SCHOOL

4. The long ī sound as in "file"

i-e says ī Compare b*i*t with b*it*e. The long ī as in "b*it*e" is spelled with (*i* + consonant + *e*), and the one consonant "t" or any other consonant is too weak between the two vowels. Therefore, the final silent "e" can still help the "i" sound like a long ī.

b*it*e	k*it*e	s*it*e	po·l*it*e
wh*it*e	wr*it*e	sp*it*e	l*ik*e
h*ik*e	b*ik*e	s*id*e	de·c*id*e
r*id*e	pr*id*e	br*id*e	t*id*e
gu*id*e	h*id*e	w*id*e	r*ip*e
w*ip*e	p*ip*e	w*if*e	l*if*e
*k*n*if*e	f*iv*e	d*iv*e	dr*iv*e
m*il*e	sm*il*e	p*il*e	f*il*e
t*im*e	l*im*e	d*im*e	n*in*e
f*in*e	de·f*in*e	l*in*e	sp*in*e
f*ir*e	h*ir*e	t*ir*e	w*ir*e
*ic*e	n*ic*e	sac·ri·f*ic*e	tw*ic*e
r*ic*e	pr*ic*e	sur·pr*is*e	w*is*e
r*is*e	gen·er·al·*iz*e	mem·o·r*iz*e	

Compare:

b*i*t, b*it*e	k*i*t, k*it*e	s*i*t, s*it*e	sp*i*t, sp*it*e
h*i*d, h*id*e	S*i*d, s*id*e	r*i*d, r*id*e	b*i*d, b*id*e
d*i*m, d*im*e	T*i*m, t*im*e	sl*i*m, sl*im*e	f*i*r, f*ir*e
p*i*n, p*in*e	f*i*n, f*in*e	d*i*n, d*in*e	d*i*nner, d*i*ner

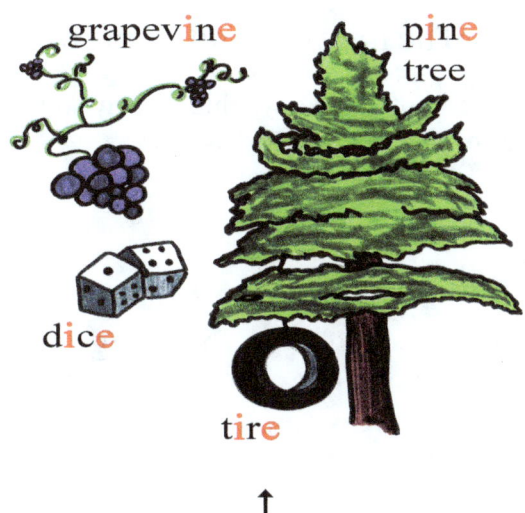

5. The long ī sound as in "style"

y-e says ī Similar to the above lesson, the long ī is spelled with (y + consonant + e), and one consonant is too weak between the two vowels (y-e).

| style | type | an·a·lyze | par·a·lyze |
| Kyle | Lyle | | |

6. The long ī sound as in "hi"

i´ says ī A stressed "i" at the end of a **first** syllable usually sounds like long ī. Read aloud and concentrate on the "i´" at the end of a stressed syllable:

hi	I	i´·ron	i·de·a
fi·nal	fi·ber	di·al	di·et
pi·lot	tri·al	bi·ol·o·gy	bi·as
bi·cy·cle	bi·lin·gual	tri·lin·gual	pri·vate
Fri·day	cri·sis	li·ar	li·on
li·cense	pli·ers	gi·ant	qui·et
Chi·na	si·lent	si·nus	vi·rus
sci·ence	Alz·hei·mer	vi·o·lin	vi·o·lent
vi·o·lence			

island

iodine

poisoned ivy

italic

7. The long ī sound as in "c**y**cle"

y´ says ī A stressed "**y**" at the end of a **first** syllable usually sounds like long **ī**. Read aloud and concentrate on the long **ī** spelled with "**y**" at the end of a stressed syllable:

c**y**´·cle	m**y**´·self	n**y**·lon	h**y**·dro·gen
h**y**·per	h**y**·phen	b**y**·pass	c**y**·ber
d**y**·nas·ty	d**y**·nam·ic	d**y**·ing	fl**y**·ing
l**y**·ing	h**y**·drau·lics		

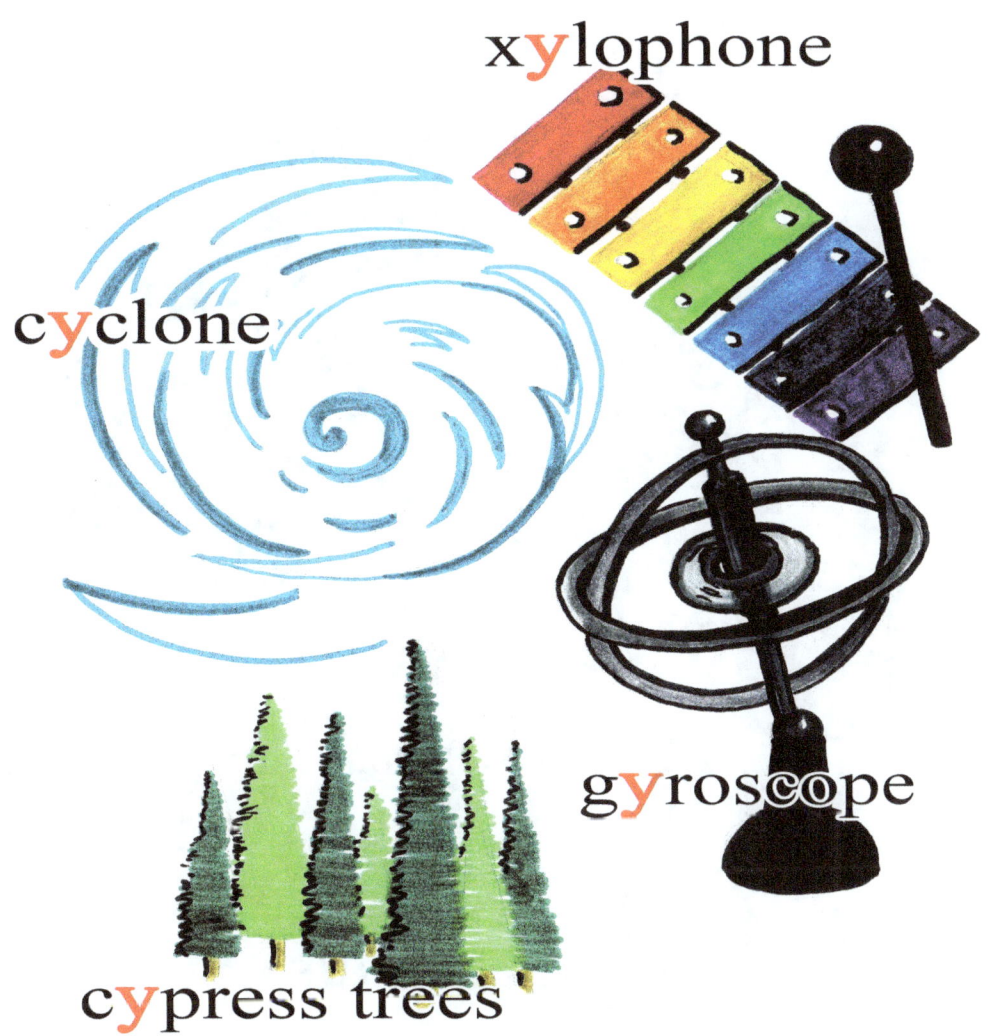

x**y**lophone

c**y**clone

g**y**roscope

c**y**press trees

8. The long ī sound as in "child"

il says ī The five semivowels **l**, **m**, **n**, **r**, and **s** make the preceding "**i**" sound long in some words. Read aloud and concentrate on the long ī spelled with "**i + semivowel**":

mild	wild	child	pint
ninth	kind	find	mind
bind	blind	rind	grind
wind	be·hind	climb	Christ
choir			

Ninth Street

child

choir

pint

wild animals

9. The long ī sound as in "die"

ie says ī When the two vowels "i" and "e" are next to each other (walking), the first one "i" does the talking and the "e" is silent. 🖐Read aloud and concentrate on the long ī spelled with "ie":

| tie | die | pie | lie |
| be·lie | un·der·lie | lied | tied |

lying

tie   pie

103

10. The long ī sound as in "dye"

ye says ī When the two vowels "**y**" and "**e**" are next to each other (walking), the "**y**" does the talking and the "**e**" is silent. 👉 Read aloud and concentrate on the long ī spelled with "**ye**":

| d**ye** | b**ye** | good-b**ye** | b**ye**-b**ye** |
| e**ye** | l**ye** | | |

hair d**ye**

eyebrows

e**ye**liner

Lesson 4: The special sounds of "i" as in "so**c**ial"

The "**i**" is no longer a vowel in these special sounds

si, ci says sh

    mis·**si**on   pa*s*·**si**on   mu·si·**ci**an   fas·**ci**sm

    a*p*·pre·**ci**at*e*

ti says sh

    ac·**ti**on   sub·stan·**ti**al   pa·**ti**enc*e*   pa·**ti**ent

di says j

    sol·**di**er

si

    vi·**si**on   tel·e·vi·**si**on   su·per·vi·**si**on

i says y

    on·**i**on   un·**i**on   be·hav·**i**or   jun·**i**or

    sen·**i**or   se·n**i**or·i·ty   fa·mi·**li**ar   pe·cu·**li**ar

    gen·**i**us

Lesson 5: The weak sound of "i" as in "test**i**fy"

The "**i**" has a weak sound in these words because it is in a syllable that is not stressed. This weak sound is called a "schwa" sound. Other syllables in a word may be stressed, but not the syllable where the schwa is:

tes´·t**i**·fy   su·**i**·cid*e*   al·**i**·mo·ny   max·**i**·mum

min·**i**·mum   a·nal·**y**·sis   a·non·**y**·mous   cous·**i**n

Homework

Say two or more words for each sound and each spelling pattern that contains:

1. The short ĭ as in sit, spill,

2. The long ī as in site, Mike,

3. The long ī as in sight,

4. The long ī as in sky,

5. The long ī as in tie,

6. The long ī as in sign,

7. The long ī as in dial,

8 The 12 Sounds of the Vowel O are Spelled in these 20 Ways

**Lesson 1:** The **12** sounds of "**O**" are spelled in **20** ways we call spelling patterns.

✓ The vowel **O** has a short sound as in "h*o*p," a long sound as in "h*o*p*e*," a special sound as in "c*ow* and "c*ou*nt," a few other special sounds as in "*o*ne," and a weak sound as in "tail*o*r."

The short **ŏ** is a unique sound that does not sound like the name of the letter **O**, and it is followed by one consonant or two, as in "st*o*p" and "st*o*pped."

The long **ō** sounds like the name of the letter **O** and it is spelled in nine spelling patterns, as in b*oa*t, t*oe*, s*ou*l, h*o*p*e*, sl*ow*, g*o*, c*o*ld, b*oy*, and b*oi*l.

107

Read Instantly by Camilia Sadik

Lesson 2: The short ŏ sound as in "hŏt"

The short ŏ is a unique sound that does not sound like the name of the letter **O**, and it is followed by one consonant or two, as in "stop" and "stopped."

Read aloud and concentrate on the one or two consonant that follow the short ŏ:

not	hot	pot	dot
lot	jot	got	hop
hopped	top	mop	stop
stopped	stop·ping	chop	shop
shopped	job	rob	robbed
rob·ber	ob·ject	prob·lem	Bob
hob·by	snob	snob·bish	Todd
odd	nod	pod	Tom
mom	com·ma	Ron	on
non	jog	jogged	log
logged	di·a·logue	locked	sock
box	fox	lodge	dodge

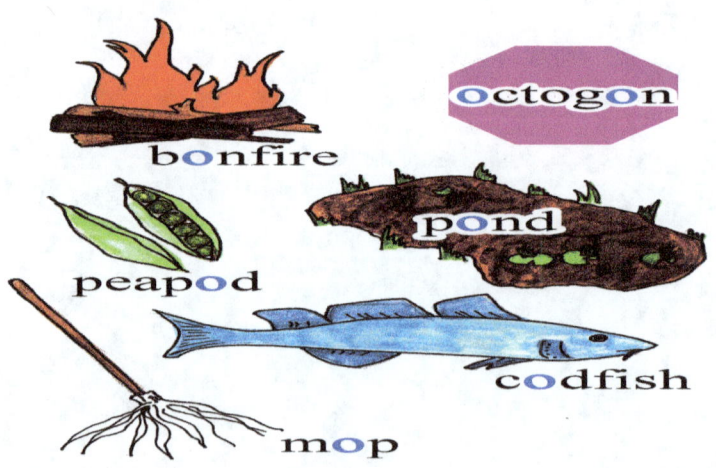

bonfire
octogon
peapod
pond
codfish
mop

Lesson 3: The long ō sound

The long ō sounds like the name of the letter **O** and it is spelled in **nine** spelling patterns, as in b**oa**t, t**oe**, s**ou**l, h**o**p**e**, sl**ow**, g**o**, c**o**ld, b**oy**, and b**oi**l.

1. The long ō sound as in "b**oa**t"

oa says ō When the two vowels "**o**" and "**a**" are walking, the first one "**o**" does the talking by saying its own letter name **O** (oh) and the second one "**a**" is silent. As with other vowels, the concept of the long "o" simply means that it can say the name of the letter **O**.

Read all the practice lessons aloud slowly and focus the vowels:

boat	coat	goat	throat
float	oat	oath	load
load·ed	up·load	toad	road
goad	loan	Joan	foam
soap	soak	soaked	coach
roach	ap·proach	goal	coal
loaf	toast	roast	coast

Compare:

got, goat	cot, coat	Todd, toad	Rod, road
John, Joan	sock, soak	cost, coast	horse, hoarse
bored, board	soar, sore		

109

2. The long ō sound as in "Joe"

oe says ō When the two vowels "oe" are walking, the first one "o" does the talking by saying its own letter name O. Saying that the "o" is long means that it can say the name of the letter O:

toe	tip·toe	Joe	foe
floe	woe	throe	doe
hoe	sloe	al·oe	o·boe

Compare:
toe, tow   floe, flow   throe, throw   sloe, slow

oboe

sloe

hoe

roe

3. The long ō sound as in "four"

 As in "four," when the two vowels "ou" are next to each other (walking), the first one "o" does the talking and the second one "u" is silent. However, the sound of long "o" is partially distorted when it is followed by an "r" as in some of these words:

four	your	pour	mourn
source	re·source	course	court
Court·ney	soul	shoul·der	dough
thor·ough			

Compare:
four, for   soul, sole   your, yore

courthouse

pour

sourdough bread

bouquet

4. The long ō sound as in "hope"

o-e says ō Compare hop with hope. As in "hope," the two vowels "o-e" can still help each other as if the one "p" between them did not exist. One consonant between two vowels is too weak; it is like having no consonant. The first vowel "o" does the talking by being a long ō and the silent "e" is there just to help the ō talk.

hope	rope	mope	cope
pope	scope	joke	broke
spoke	Coke	choke	smoke
stroke	robe	globe	note
vote	wrote	quote	cote
re·mote	pro·mote	dote	code
mode	ex·plode	ep·i·sode	owe
throne	phone	tone	stone
cone	bone	clone	a·lone
zone	home	Rome	nose
hose	chose	rose	pose
sup·pose	en·closed	close	clothes
dose	doze	froze	drove
grove	stove	role	pa·role
hole	whole	sole	pole

Compare:

hop, hope	hopping, hoping	mop, mope
cop, cope	pop, pope	not, note
dot, dote	cot, cote	rob, robe
cod, code	com·ma, co·ma	jock, joke
Ross, rose	Sol, sole, soul	throne, thrown

cologne

gnome

jump rope

chromosomes

garlic clove

5. The long ō sound as in "snow"

ow says ō As in "snow," the "ow" makes the long ō sound. This pattern is useful to tell apart words like "tow" and "toe." Notice that this "ow" phonic is mainly found at the end of words:

snow	show	sow	tow
know	row	grow	bow
mow	low	slow·ly	flow
glow	blow	throw	yel·low
pil·low	fol·low	nar·row	to·mor·row
known	shown	own	bowl

 Compare:
| tow, toe | flow, floe | throw, throe | know, no |
| thrown, throne | sow, so | slow, sloe | |

rainbow, window, bowling, lawnmower, meadow, snow, yellow wheelbarrow

6. The long ō sound as in "go"

o′· says ō The stressed "o′" at the end of a syllable makes a long ō sound. Read aloud slowly and always concentrate your vision on the vowels:

no′	so′	so′-so′	go′
hel·lo′	so′·lo′	yo′-yo′	ze·ro′
he·ro′	in·tro′	pho′·to′	au·to′
ve·to′	o′·pen	o′·kay	o′·dor
do′·nor	po′·et·ry	mo′·tive	mo′·tion
no′·tice	no′·ble	so′·fa	

Compare:
no, know   so, sow

Plato   silo

sofa

mocha   cello

115

7. The long ō sound as in "for"

ō + semivowel Because the **l**, **m**, **n**, **r** and **s** are semivowels, they can sometimes act like vowels. In this case they can make the preceding "o" a long ō as in the following words:

ōr

for	for·ty	form	for·mal
cor·ner	or·der	nor·mal	porch
torch	air·port	short	lord
cord	cork	fork	born
corn	horse	force	forced

ōl

old	cold	gold	hold
told	bold	fold	sold
sol·dier	bolt	scroll	poll
toll	roll	en·roll	con·trol
swol·len	yolk	folk	pol·ka
up·hol·ster·y			

ōs

most	post	host	host·ess
ghost	gross	post·age	os·trich
as·bes·tos			

ōm

comb

Compare:
roll, role   poll, pole   for, four

Chapter 8: Phonics Made by O

8. The long ō sound as in "bōy"

oy says ōy The sound of "oy" as in "bōy" and "oi" as in "bōil" is the same special sound of long ō—usually, the "oy" is for the end of words, and the "oi" is for inside words:

ōy

boy	soy	toy	troy
joy	en·joy	Roy	em·ploy
de·ploy	des·troy	loy·al	an·noy

 Compare:
    boy, boil   soy, soil   toy, toil   coy, coil

oysters

toy boat

soy milk

9. The long ō sound as in "boil"

oi says ōi The sound of "oi" as in "boil" and "oy" as in "boy" is the same special sound of long ō—usually, the "oy" is for the end of words, and the "oi" is for inside words:

ōi

oil	boil	toil	coil
foil	soil	spoil	broil
coin	join	loin	joints
point	void	a·void	voice
choice	noise	poi·son	moist

Chapter 8: Phonics Made by O

Lesson 4: The special sound of "o" as in "n**o**w" and as in "n**ou**n"

Compare:
    fl**ow**·er, fl**ou**r   f**ow**l, f**ou**l   **ou**r, h**ou**r

ow The special sound of "o" as in "c**ow**" is mainly for the end of words. Read aloud:

c**ow**	h**ow**	n**ow**	pl**ow**
b**ow**	ch**ow**	D**ow**	fl**ow**·er
p**ow**·er	t**ow**·el	v**ow**·el	**ow**l
c**ow**l	f**ow**l	gr**ow**l	cr**ow**d
dr**ow**n	d**ow**n·t**ow**n	sh**ow**·er	t**ow**·er

c**ow**boy hat

c**ow**

owl

sunfl**ow**ers

ou The special sound of "o" as in "out" is mainly for inside words:

fl**ou**r	**our**	h*our*	**out**
sh**ou**t	s**ou**th	m**ou**th	c**ou**ch
n**ou**n	gr**ou**nd	im·p**ou**nd	f**ou**nd
c**ou**nt	ac·c**ou**nt	c**ou**n·ty	l**ou**d
a·l**ou**d	cl**ou**d	h**ou**se	m**ou**se
m**ou**n·tain	f**ou**n·tain	bl**ou**se	f**ou**l

tr**ou**sers

b**ou**ghs

tr**ou**t

bean spr**ou**ts

Chapter 8: Phonics Made by O

Lesson 5: The minor sounds of "o" as in "wood"

oo The "oo" has this special sound that occurs in a small number of words:

wood	good	stood	hood
neighbor·hood	child·hood	book	cook
look	took	hook	shook

Compare:
wood, would   [could, should]

o says w The "o" in these words is no longer a vowel but it sounds like the consonant "w":

| one | once | ones | choir |
| res·er·voir | rep·er·toire | mem·oir | Ren·oir |

silent o The "o" is silent in a few words:

touch	Doug	dou·ble	cou·ple
jour·nal	ad·journ	you	boul·e·vard
peo·ple	sub·poe·na		

ou says au The "ou" in these words sounds like the "au" as in "taught." Note how all these examples contain the "gh," which serves to modulate the "ou":

| bought | brought | fought |
| sought | thought | ought |

121

Lesson 6: Weak sound of "o" as in "fav o r"

The unstressed, weak sound of "o" is called a schwa sound. Notice how other syllables may be stressed but not the syllable where the schwa is. Read aloud slowly:

gov'·er·n o r	do'·n o r	ven'·d o r	ra'·z o r
fa'·v o r	sail'· o r	tai'·l o r	coun'·sel· o r
coun'·cil· o r	pro'·fes·s o r	ed·u'·ca·t o r	ob·tain'
o ·pin·ion'	s o ·lic·it'	mem· o ·ry'	ob·nox'·ious
ba l '·l o t			

Homework

Say two or more words for each sound and each spelling pattern that contains:

1. The short ŏ as in hot, cop,

2. The long ō as in boat, foam,

3. The long ō as in hope, note,

4. The long ō as in toe, soul

5. The long ō as in snow,

6. The "oy" and "oi" as in boy, boil,

7. The "ow" and "ou" as in flower, flour,

8. The "oo" as in zoo, wood,

Chapter 9: Phonics Made by U

The 6 Sounds of the Vowel U are Spelled in these 28 Ways

Lesson 1: The **six** sounds of "u" are spelled in **28** ways we call spelling patterns

✓ The vowel **U** has a short sound as in "c**u**t," a long sound as in "c**u**te," other minor sounds as in "q**u**een," and a weak sound as in "mi′·n**u**s."

The short **ŭ** is a unique sound that does not sound like the name of the letter **U**, and it is spelled with one or two consonant after it as in "**u**p" and "**u**pper."

The long **ū** sounds like the name of the letter **U**. The long **ū** has two slightly different sounds and they are **yoo** as in "contin**ue**" and **oo** as in "bl**ue**." The long **ū** sound is spelled in **nine** spelling patterns, as in bl**ue**, s**ui**t, c**u**te, f**eu**d, f**ew**, y**ou**, h**u**man, d**o**, and z**oo**.

Read Instantly by Camilia Sadik

Lesson 2: The short ŭ sound as in "up"

 The short ŭ is a unique sound that does not sound like the name of the letter **U**, and it is followed by one or two consonant, as in "**u**p" and "**u**pper." Read aloud slowly:

up	**u**s	c**u**p	c**u**t
c**u**t·ter	**u**p·per	s**u**p·per	b**u**t
sh**u**t	h**u**t	n**u**ts	b**u**s
r**u**b	t**u**b	st**u**b	cl**u**b
scr**u**b	scr**u**bb**e**d	B**u**d	m**u**d
s**u**d·den	f**u**n	r**u**n	s**u**n
n**u**n	r**u**g	h**u**g	h**u**gg**e**d
pl**u**g	pl**u**gg**e**d	pl**u**g·ging	pl**u**ck
pl**u**ck**e**d	l**u**ck	tr**u**ck	dr**u**m
b**u**m	th**u**mb	cr**u**mb	pl**u**m·ber
j**u**mp	j**u**dge	m**u**ch	cl**u**tch

chubby puppy
hummingbird
bubble bath
duck
bunny

124

Chapter 9: Phonics Made by U

Note: In a limited number of words, the short ŭ sound is spelled with o, ou, or ui as in:

o says ŭ

oth·er	ov·en	some	come
son	none	done	Mon·day
flood	blood		

ou says ŭ

touch	in touch	dou·ble	trou·ble
cou·ple	Doug	cous·in	boul·e·vard
rough	e·nough	tough	coun·try
doubt	build	built	

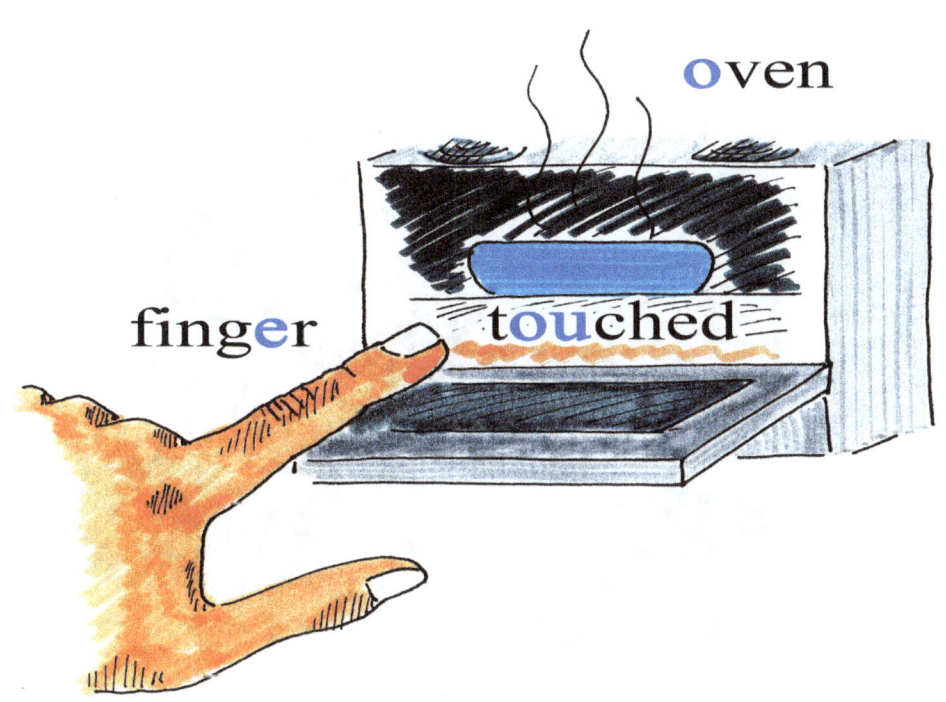

Read Instantly by Camilia Sadik

Lesson 3: The long ū sound

The long ū sounds like the name of the letter **U**. The long ū has two slightly different sounds and they are **yoo** as in "contin**ue**" and **oo** as in "bl**ue**." The long ū sound is spelled in nine spelling patterns, as in bl**ue**, s**ui**t, c**u**te, f**eu**d, f**ew**, y**ou**, h**u**man, d**o**, and z**oo**.

1. The long ū sound as in "bl**ue**"

ue says ū When the two vowels "**u**" and "**e**" are next to each other (walking), the first one "**u**" does the talking by saying its own letter name **U** and the second one "**e**" is silent. Read all the practice lessons aloud slowly:

bl**ue**	cl**ue**	gl**ue**	fl**ue**
d**ue**	res·i·d**ue**	ar·g**ue**	tr**ue**
s**ue**	pur·s**ue**	vir·t**ue**	stat·**ue**
T**ue**s·day	is·s**ue**	tis·s**ue**	en·s**ue**
con·tin·**ue**	ven·**ue**	res·c**ue**	res·c**ue**d

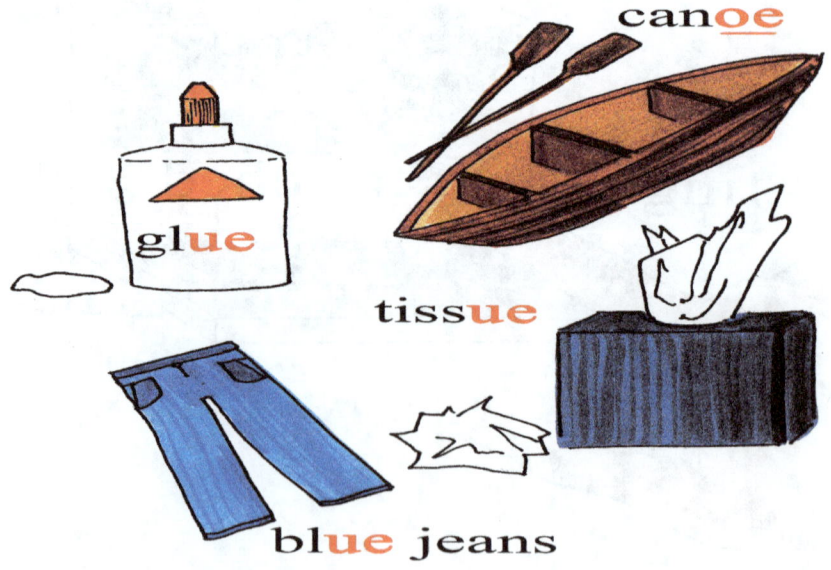

can**oe**

gl**ue**

tis**sue**

bl**ue** jeans

2. The long ū sound as in "suit"

ui says ū When the two vowels "u" and "i" are next to each other (walking), the first one "u" does the talking by saying its own letter name **U** and the second one "i" is silent.

fruit	juice	bruise	cruise
re·cruit	suit	pur·suit	suit·a·ble
suit·case	law·suit		

Compare:
pur·sue, pur·suit

fruit juice

conduit

suit

3. The long ū sound as in "cute"

u-e says ū Compare cut, cute. As in "cute," the two vowels "u-e" can still help each other as if the one "t" between them did not exist. One "t" between two vowels is too weak; it is like having no consonant between "u" and "e." This explains the cause for doubling the consonants; it is to be strong enough to keep the vowels from helping each other.

cute	mute	chute	brute
jute	lute	flute	in·clude
rude	crude	tube	cube
rule	mule	fume	per·fume
June	tune	prune	use
fuse	ex·cuse	muse	Duke
huge	truce	Bruce	re·duce
pro·duce	sure	in·sur·ance	cure

Compare:
| cut, cute | cut·ter, cu·ter | tub, tube | sup·per, su·per |

flute

computer

sugar

prune

Chapter 9: Phonics Made by U

4. The long ū sound as in "feud"

eu says ū The long **ū** is spelled with "**eu**" as in "f**eu**d," "**ew**" as in "f**ew**," and "**ou**" as in "gr**ou**p." In these three unusual cases when two vowels are walking, it is the **second** one that does the talking and the first one is silent. Perhaps various spelling patterns of the same sound are used to tell apart word that sound the same but have different meanings (homonyms).

Eu·rop*e*	*Eu*·ro·pe·an	*eu*·lo·gy	f*eu*d
n*eu*·tral	n*eu*·rol·o·gist	d*eu*ce	l*eu*·ke·mia
l*ieu*·ten·ant	*Eu*·gene	*Eu*·nice	Z*eu*s
en·tre·pre·n*eur*	gran·d*eur*	chau*f*·f*eur*	*p*s*eu*·do
r*heu*·ma·tism	b*eau*·ti·ful		

5. The long ū sound as in "few"

ew says ū The long **ū** is spelled with "**ew**" as in "f**ew**," and the "**w**" is a vowel in this case. Think of the name of "w" as "double **u** = **uu**" and connect that to the fact that the "**w**" sounds like the vowel "u" in this case. Perhaps this "**ew**" pattern was originally used to tell apart two words like "d**ew**" and "d**ue**," and once the pattern was used, more words ended up being spelled with it.

f*ew*	n*ew*	*k*n*ew*	n*ew*s
fl*ew*	bl*ew*	st*ew*	st*ew*ed
st*ew*·ing	dr*ew*	gr*ew*	cr*ew*
scr*ew*	scr*ew*·driver	br*ew*	br*ew*·er·y
cl*ew*	d*ew*	ch*ew*	thr*ew*
shr*ew*	shr*ew*d	l*ew*d	h*ew*
p*ew*	sp*ew*	m*ew*	cur·f*ew*
neph·*ew*	d*ew*	j*ew*·el	j*ew*·els
j*ew*·el·ry	[v*iew*	re·v*iew*	in·ter·v*iew*]

Read Instantly by Camilia Sadik

 Compare the following examples of such homonyms:

cl**ue**, cl**ew**　　　　bl**ue**, bl**ew**　　　　d**ue**, d**ew**

thr**ew**, thr**ough**　　　r**ou**te, r**ou**t　　　tr**ou**pe, tr**oo**p

6. The long ū sound as in "menu"

u´ · says ū As in "hu´·man," a stressed u´ at the end of a syllable sounds like long ū.

men·u´	fl**u**	h**u**´·man	s**u**·per
t**u**·tor	**u**·ter·us	**u**·nit	**u**·ni·ver·si·ty
u·su·al	**u**·su·al·ly	U-turn	d**u**·el
f**u**·el	cr**u**·el	fl**u**·ent	grad·**u**·ate
r**u**·in	fl**u**·id	t**u**·i·tion	con·tin·**u**·ous
d**u**·ty	f**u**·ture	in·sti·t**u**·tion	n**u**·tri·tion
J**u**·pi·ter	com·p**u**·ter	st**u**·di·o	J**u**·dy
st**u**·dent	l**u**·nar	h**u**·mor	h**u**·mor·ous
m**u**·se·um	m**u**·sic	m**u**·si·cian	fac·t**u**·al
ac·t**u**·al	in·tel·lec·t**u**·al	ha·bit·**u**·al	sit·**u**·ate

131

7. The long ū sound as in to, too, you, and wood

O says ū The long ū is spelled with O's in a small number of words. Perhaps such various spelling patterns were used to tell apart words that sounded the same.

 Compare the following examples of such homonyms:

do, due, dew   troop, troupe   wood, would

to, too, two

7. Long ū as in "who"

O says ū

do	to	in·to	who
two	whom	womb	tomb
move	im·prove	[wood	good]

132

8. The long ū sound as in "z**oo**"

oo says ū

z**oo**	t**oo**	sh**oo**	ta·b**oo**
sham·p**oo**	b**oo**ts	r**oo**t	sh**oo**t
c**oo**l	f**oo**l	p**oo**l	sch**oo**l
w**oo**l	r**oo**m	br**oo**m	gr**oo**m
z**oo**m	n**oo**n	ba*l*·l**oo**n	s**oo**n
sp**oo**n	m**oo**s*e*	g**oo**s*e*	l**oo**s*e*
r**oo**st·*er*	ch**oo**s*e*	f**oo**d	m**oo**d
r**oo**f	pr**oo**f	gr**oo**v*e*	sm**oo**th
t**oo**th	b**oo**th		

133

9. The long ū sound as in "you"

oū

| you | youth | through | group |
| soup | troupe | coup | route |

10. The long ū sound as in "book"

oo

wood	good	stood	hood
neigh·bor·hood	child·hood	book	cook
look	took	hook	shook

Chapter 9: Phonics Made by U

Lesson 4: The special sounds of "u": "cul**ture**, liq**u**id, g**u**est, b**u**siness"

-ture The suffix "**-ture**" has this special sound. Read aloud slowly:

fur·ni·**ture**	sig·na·**ture**	ad·ven·**ture**	ag·ri·cul·**ture**
vul·**ture**	fu·**ture**	na·**ture**	min·i·a·**ture**
cap·**ture**	rup·**ture**	frac·**ture**	lec·**ture**
struc·**ture**	ac·u·punc·**ture**	de·par·**ture**	lit·er·a·**ture**
ges·**ture**	mois·**ture**	fea·**ture**	ven·**ture**

u says W The "u" is not a vowel in these words because it sounds like the consonant "**w**":

q**u**ick	liq·**u**id	re·q**u**est	ban·q**u**et
q**u**een	e·q**u**al	s**u**ite	s**u**ave
s**u**ede	per·s**u**ade	c**u**i·sine	lan·g**u**age
bi·lin·g**u**al	tri·lin·g**u**al	dis·tin·g**u**ish	ex·tin·g**u**ish·er
ac·q**u**aint	ac·q**u**ain·tan·ces		

silent *u* The silent "*u*" in some of these words is to keep the "**g**" hard:

g**u**est	g**u**ess	g**u**i·tar	g**u**ild
g**u**ilt	dis·g**u**ise	g**u**ide	g**u**ile
g**u**y	g**u**ard	g**u**ar·an·tee	leag**u**e
cat·a·log**u**e	g**u**e·ril·la	u·niq**u**e	tech·niq**u**e
an·tiq**u**e			

u says ĭ The "u" sounds like short ĭ in these two words:
    b**u**si·ness   b**u**s·y

Lesson 5: The weak sound of "u" as in "vi′·rus"

ə The unstressed, weak sound of "u" is called a schwa sound. Because this sound is weak, it can be confused with other vowels' sounds:

mi′·nus	si·nus	bo·nus
vi·rus	u·ter·us	fo·cus
cir·cus	gen·ius	Sat·ur·day
in·jury	mil·len·ni·um	sta·di·um
mu·se·um	cur·ric·u·lum	

us says ə The -us at the end of these adjectives has a single weak sound of the vowel "u," called a schwa sound:

vi·rus	u·ter·us	si·nus	mi·nus
bo·nus	syl·la·bus	stim·u·lus	gen·ius
ra·di·us	Cel·si·us		

ous says ə The -ous at the end of these adjectives has a single weak sound of the vowel "u," called a schwa sound:

mar·vel·ous	jeal·ous	fab·u·lous	ri·dic·u·lous
con·tin·u·ous	am·big·u·ous	nerv·ous	glam·or·ous
hu·mor·ous	rig·or·ous	gen·er·ous	num·er·ous
pros·per·ous	dan·ger·ous	pre·pos·ter·ous	cu·ri·ous
se·ri·ous	var·i·ous	ob·vi·ous	con·ta·gious
cour·te·ous	gor·geous	cou·ra·geous	out·ra·geous
si·mul·ta·ne·ous	mis·cel·la·ne·ous		

Lesson 6: Review of old and new phonics

The following lessons are old and new phonics. Sometimes the letters **c**, **s**, and **t** can join with a following vowel and cause that vowel to lose its vowel sound, especially at the end of words or at the end of syllables. For instance, the "**tu**" in "**ture**" as in "cul**tu**re" becomes a single sound.

Read aloud slowly:

ac·**tion**	auc·**tion**	ed·u·ca·**tion**
ex·pres·**sion**	mis·**sion**	ad·mis·**sion**
mu·si·**cian**	phy·si·**cian**	pol·it·i·**cian**
e·lec·tri·**cian**	sus·pi·**cion**	o·**cean**
sugar	**sur**e	in·**sure**
tis·**sue**	is·**sue**	is·**sue**s
en·**sue**	**Se**an	con·tro·ver·**sial**
so·**cia**l	fa·**cia**l	spe·**cia**l
ar·ti·fi·**cia**l	cru·**cia**l	de·li·**ci**ous
sus·pi·**ci**ous	pre·**ci**ous	Fe·li·**cia**
x=**kc**→	an**x**·ious	ob·no**x**·ious
am·bi·**ti**ous	su·per·sti·**ti**ous	fic·ti·**ti**ous
pa·**ti**ent	ra·**ti**o	sub·stan·**tia**l
con·fi·den·**tia**l	res·i·den·**tia**l	in·i·**tia**l
pres·**sure**	pres·**sure**d	cen·**sure**

plea·sure	trea·sure	mea·sure
mea·sure·ment	u·su·al	u·su·al·ly
vi·sion	in·va·sion	in·tru·sion
de·ci·sion	Cau·ca·sian	am·ne·sia
pro·ce·dure	re·sid·u·als	ed·u·cate
sched·ule	mod·ule	sol·dier
fur·ni·ture	sig·na·ture	cul·ture
ag·ri·cul·ture	fu·ture	tem·per·a·ture
lec·ture	[am·a·teur]	bap·tism
so·cial·ism	cap·i·tal·ism	re·al·ism
jus·ti·fy	qual·i·fy	no·ti·fy
cit·y	eth·nic·i·ty	ve·loc·i·ty
u·ni·ver·si·ty	o·be·si·ty	an·i·mos·i·ty
rel·a·tive	ac·tive	con·struc·tive
pos·i·tive	at·trac·tive	de·duc·tive
fu·gi·tive	cog·ni·tive	bi·ol·o·gy
psy·chol·o·gy	neu·rol·o·gy	an·thro·pol·o·gy

10

Writing the ABC's

Lesson 1: Now is the time to write the ABC's

Only after reading this entire book aloud, begin to write. Use a lined piece of paper to practice writing the ABC's in lowercase and then in uppercase. Be sure to begin by writing the lowercase first. Notice the five letters g, j, p, q and y extend below the line:

a   b   c   d   e   f   g

h   i   j   k   l   m   n

o   p   q   r   s   t   u

v   w   x   y   z

Read Instantly by Camilia Sadik

📘 Practice writing the ABC's in uppercase. Notice that uppercase Q extends below the line:

A   B   C   D   E   F   G

H   I   J   K   L   M   N

O   P   Q   R   S   T   U

V   W   X   Y   Z

📘 Practice writing these six letters that extend below the line:

g   j   p

q   y   Q

Chapter 10: Writing the ABC's

✒ Practice writing the ABC's in cursive lowercase:

a   *b*   *c*   *d*   *e*

f   *g*   *h*   *i*   *j*

k   *l*   *m*   *n*   *o*

p   *q*   *r*   *s*   *t*

u   *v*   *w*   *x*   *y*

z

Read Instantly by Camilia Sadik

Practice writing the ABC's in cursive lowercase using a different font:

a   b   c   d   e

f   g   h   i   j

k   l   m   n   o

p   q   r   s   t

u   v   w   x   y

z

Chapter 10: Writing the ABC's

✎ Practice writing the ABC's in cursive uppercase:

A   *B*   *C*   *D*   *E*

F   *G*   *H*   *I*   *J*

K   *L*   *M*   *N*   *O*

P   *Q*   *R*   *S*   *T*

U   *V*   *W*   *X*   *Y*

Z

Read Instantly by Camilia Sadik

Practice writing the ABC"s in cursive uppercase using a different font:

A   *B*   *C*   *D*   *E*

F   *G*   *H*   *I*   *J*

K   *L*   *M*   *N*   *O*

P   *Q*   *R*   *S*   *T*

U   *V*   *W*   *X*   *Y*

Z

The 10 Phonics-based Spelling Books for all Ages by Linguist Camilia Sadik

Book 1: *Read Instantly* - 200 Logical Phonics Lessons for all Ages

This book is to teach phonics, and in it lies the groundwork for learning the rules that govern phonics. Anyone capable of learning the ABC's is guaranteed to learn to read from this book. Each vowel is dissected and isolated in a chapter in the second half of this book. Parents can now teach reading before sending kids to schools. This book is for beginners, but all learners need to start with it to learn phonics in a brand-new way.

Book 2: *Learn to Spell 500 Words a Day* (6 volumes: A, E, I, O, U, Consonants)

Vowels are inconsistent, they rule English, and they cannot be avoided. In this book, each vowel is dissected and isolated in a volume. The eight consonants c, g, h, q, s, x, w, and y are also inconsistent; and they are isolated in a volume. Each lesson begins with a spelling rule, followed by a list of the words that follow that rule, followed by comprehensive and detailed practice lessons, and students are asked to read aloud to memorize the spelling of hundreds of words at a time. This book is for the intermediate level, ideal for grades 4-12 and for adult learners.

Book 3: *100 Spelling Rules*

Each spelling rule in this book is followed by a list of nearly all the words that follow it. Advanced students learn to spell hundreds of words from this book. Sadik's books are cumulative, and the book *100 Spelling Rules* is a book for the advance level.

Book 4: *The Compound Words* - 7,000 Compound and Hyphenated Words

Unlike looking up words in a dictionary, over 5,000 compound words and 2,000 hyphenated words are isolated in this book, grouped alphabetically, colored, and prepared for adults and children to read and learn. As in "rustproof," a compound word is composed of two or more words. As in "face-to-face," a hyphenated word is made of the two or more words, separated by hyphens.

Book 5: *Teachers' Guide*

This guide is for teachers, parents, or adult learners. It contains explanations of the methodology and the symbols and concepts used in the books. It contains dyslexia solutions, spelling tests, and more. *Read more*   SpellingRules.com →

How to purchase books by Camilia Sadik

SpellingRules.com   Amazon.com   Bookstores Worldwide

About the Author

Linguist Camilia Sadik spent 15 years intensely dissecting English, discovering over 100 spelling rules, applying the rules in 600 phonics-based spelling lessons, class-testing her discoveries and preparing learning books for children and adults to read and spell hundreds of words at a time. The 30 unique learning features in Sadik's book make learning to read and spell inescapable. Sadik worked hard to make spelling easy and possible for all ages and all types of learners. In addition, Sadik found an easy solution to end dyslexia in spelling and in writing letters in reverse. Learning to spell and slowing down to write words slowly ends dyslexia.

Sadik saw the details of English sounds and their various spelling patterns and used that in easy-to-use vowels and consonants books. See these examples:

The vowel **A** has 5 sounds that are spelled in 12 ways.

The vowel **E** has 7 sounds that are spelled in 17 ways.

The vowel **I** has 8 sounds that are spelled in 19 ways.

The vowel **O** has 12 sounds that are spelled in 20 ways.

The vowel **U** has 6 sounds that are spelled in 28 ways.

Eight **consonants** have 50 sounds that are spelled in 60 ways.

Academically, Sadik earned a BA in Philosophy from WSU and an MA in Applied Linguistics from SDSU. In addition, Sadik earned California Teaching Credentials and is certified in teaching ABE and ESL. Before writing books, Sadik spent over 10 years reading the best of the world's literature.

©1997 Camilia Sadik

All rights reserved. Camilia Sadik patented each new spelling rule she discovered. Printed in the United States of America, and except as permitted under the United States Copyright Act of 1976. No part of this publication may be reproduced or distributed in any form or by any means, or stored in a database retrieval system, without prior written permission of the publisher.

www.ingramcontent.com/pod-product-compliance
Lightning Source LLC
Chambersburg PA
CBHW081358290426
44110CB00018B/2409